The Americanization of Germany, 1945–1949

For West Germany, life in the aftermath of war was marked by the overwhelming presence of the occupying forces. In his study of the American Occupation and its influence on German post-war life and culture, Ralph Willett traces the origins of the economic miracle which was to come, focusing not on the political and economic regeneration of Germany, but on its cultural reconstruction.

Tracing Germany's gradual, and uneasy, acceptance of American imperialism, Willett's study encompasses the effects of such icons of modernity as popular movies, art and architecture, fiction, drama and the survival of the jazz movement, Coca-Cola and automobiles. The book explores how these images of efficiency and consumerism, and the Cold War propaganda which accompanied them, led to the inevitable birth of the modern capitalist society and throws fascinating light on the subsequently far-reaching phenomenon of 'Coca-Colonization'.

'Elegantly written, often fascinating in its details, whether those are German adverts for Coca-Cola, the illuminating fact of the Deutschmark's similarity to the American dollar (the US mint printed both), or the story of jazz's survival under the Nazis.'

Here

'Willett takes us on a Wim  var-
ravaged cityscapes of Germa thy
the atmosphere in which Am ely
materialist ideology fell upon
Social Hist sity

The author: Ralph Willett is the
University of Hull. He has also taught at Hofstra University, New York; American University, Washington DC; and the University of Alabama. In recent articles he has examined popular music in wartime Germany, and American popular culture and consumption.

Studies in film, television and the media

General Editor: Dr Anthony Aldgate
The Open University

Cinema, Literature and Society: Elite and Mass Culture in Interwar Britain
Peter Miles and Malcolm Smith

The Americanization of Germany, 1945–1949
Ralph Willett

European Cinemas, European Societies 1939–1990
Pierre Sorlin

The Americanization of Germany, 1945–1949

Ralph Willett

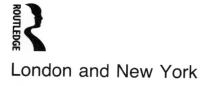

London and New York

First published in 1989
by Routledge

First published in paperback in 1992
by Routledge
11 New Fetter Lane, London EC4P 4EE

Simultaneously published in the USA and Canada
by Routledge
a division of Routledge, Chapman and Hall Inc.
29 West 35th Street, New York, NY 10001

Printed in Great Britain by Hartnolls Ltd, Bodmin, Cornwall.

British Library Cataloguing-in-Publication Data
Willett, Ralph
  The americanization of Germany, 1945–1949.
  (Studies in film, television and the media.
  ISSN 0955–8594)
  I. Title   II. Series
  942.0874

American Library of Congress Data also available

  ISBN 0–415–07710–9

Contents

List of Plates		vi
Preface		viii
Acknowledgements		x
Abbreviations		xi
1	**Cultural Interactions and Perceptions in the American Zone**	1
2	**Re-education: 'Your Job in Germany'**	16
3	**Film: The Affair of Billy Wilder's** *A Foreign Affair*	28
4	**Art and Architecture: From Wasteland to Late Modernism**	45
5	**Fiction and Drama: That's Entertainment!**	54
6	**Magazines: Fantasy Unlimited**	73
7	**Jazz: The Sound of Democracy**	86
8	**Coca-Cola and Cars: Icons of the American Dream**	99
9	**The 1950s: Cold War / Hot Sun in Capri**	115
	Notes	132
	Select Bibliography	141
	Post-war Chronology	147
	Index	149

List of Plates

Plate 1   Coca-Cola advertisement, courtesy of
                   Coca-Cola Nachrichten (News), January
                   1950, p.11

Plates 2 and 3 Scenes from Wilder's *A Foreign Affair*,
                   Paramount 1948, courtesy of the National
                   Film Archive, London

Plates 4 and 5 Photographs of Germany, courtesy of Klaus
                   Jaeger and Helmut Regel (eds), *Deutschland
                   in Trümmern: Film Dokumente der Jahre
                   1945–1949, Oberhausen, 1976*

The US occupation zone

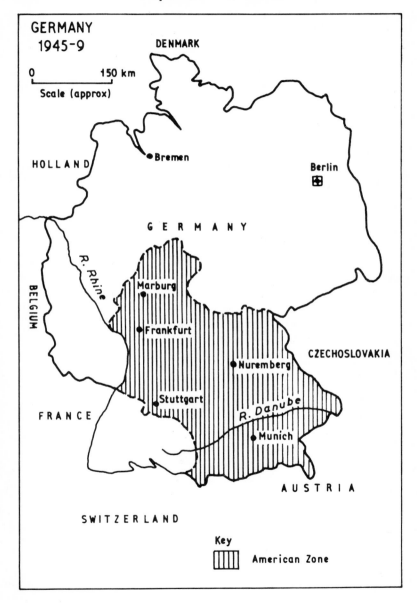

GERMANY
1945-9

0   150 km
Scale (approx)

DENMARK

HOLLAND

● Bremen

Berlin

GERMANY

R. Rhine

BELGIUM

Marburg
●

● Frankfurt

CZECHOSLOVAKIA

● Nuremberg

Stuttgart
●

R. Danube

FRANCE

● Munich

AUSTRIA

SWITZERLAND

Key
American Zone

Preface

In the summer of 1986 I visited the small resort of La Tranche-sur-mer on the west coast of France. Visitors were smoking Marlboros and drinking Coca-Cola, and *Rocky IV* was playing at the local cinema. On the other hand the food bought at open-air markets and eaten in restaurants and hotels was unmistakably French, as were the touring circus, the folklore groups, the local Parade of Flowers, and, inland, the rural life and customs of the marshes. Americanization has of course affected French life, visibly during the 1960s, but it has been carried out with French discrimination and style, acknowledging a difference between Americanization and modernization.

Germany by contrast offers a case study of a deeper and more pervasive version of a cultural imperialism now experienced throughout the world. From the time the theatres and cinemas reopened amidst the rubble of post-war Berlin, Americanization has grown from a trickle to a flood. The reasons advanced for this phenomenon are various, but a beginning can be made with the circumstance of *Stunde Null* (Zero Hour) in 1945, when a social and cultural vacuum had been created. American influence, however, had existed before the war by means of design, movies, jazz, and so on.[1] Subjected to Nazi propaganda for over a decade, many Germans regarded the imposition of re-education cynically. Yet the extent of the programme ensured some impact upon an indigenous population which was unwilling to confront the past. Fascism and its totalitarian counterpart, Communism, were unacceptable – so, from the point of view of the victors, the way was clear for 'democracy'. That official influence may well have been transcended by what resulted from the sheer presence of the

Occupation forces: GIs were both welcome and reviled but evidence of their culture, traced in the following pages, became increasingly inescapable.

The aims of this book are modest: its basis is a short period of time (though one in which foreign policy imperatives hardened American attitudes towards Europe and Germany) and it does not attempt to cover all areas of Americanization. Its chapter about films focuses on a movie which, during the Occupation, was forbidden in Germany. However, Americanization is revealed as much by what it avoids as by what it promotes or encourages. Further, this study has no conclusion since one was provided by history: the economic miracle of the fifties. What led up to that explosion of affluence and consumerism is itself fascinating and of interest to all who have witnessed the global process of 'Coca-Colonization'.

Acknowledgements

Having conformed to a set of prescriptions for an academic preface – disclaimers, qualifications, and professions of humility – I now proceed to the usual effusive thanks offered to friends, colleagues, and spouse. My strategy in fulfilling these rules (originally announced in *PMLA* but reiterated by David Lodge) is actually to generate in the main text that coherence and confident monologism by which, it is claimed, authors are characteristically dismayed.

Above all, I must thank the Research Institute at the University of Siegen, West Germany, where I spent a sabbatical semester in 1984. Chapter Three appeared in a different version in *The Historical Journal of Film, Radio and Television*, vol. 7, no. 1, 1987; my thanks go to its editor, Ken Short, for generous, friendly assistance at all stages of the 'Wilder project'. I am especially grateful to Professor Drost, Frau Krebs, and my old friend, Professor Christian Thomsen. I should like to list, in no particular order, all those who have rendered assistance, if only the provision of a room, a bed, beer, and conversation somewhere in Germany: Tony McCobb, Brewster Chamberlin, Fred Ritzel, Hans Wolfschutz, Erika Carter, Ken Short, Armin Guntermann, Phil and Guerdal Mothershaw, Karl Riha, Simon Frith, Brenda West, Robin Headlam Wells, Bruce Crowther, Heinz Ickstadt, Volker Berghahn, Dr Hilges at Coca-Cola GmbH, Essen, Michael Hoenisch, and Armin Fuchs. If this list were in order, at the top, for dozens of reasons (including her Raspberry Pavlova) would be Jean Willett.

Abbreviations

AFN	Armed Forces Network
CARE	Co-operation for American Remittance to Europe
CRALOG	Committee of Relief Agencies Licensed to Operate in Germany
OMGUS	The Office of Military Government United States
OWI	Office of War Information
SPD	Social Democratic Party
USIC	US Information Center

Chapter one

Cultural Interactions and Perceptions in the American Zone[1]

> I hear you say:
> He talks about America.
> He doesn't understand anything about it
> He was never there.
> But believe me
> You understand me very well when I talk about America.
> And the best thing about America is:
> That we understand it.
>> (Bertolt Brecht, 'Reader for Big-City Dwellers', c.1926,
>> *Collected Works* [Frankfurt/Main, 1967], VIII, p. 286)

> What's German culture? These days it's American culture
> – the same books, the same music, the same movies,
> even the same clothes. They've bought us wholesale and
> they have the nerve to sneer.
>> (Paul Theroux, 'Volunteer Speaker' in *The London
>> Embassy* [Penguin, Harmondsworth, 1983], p. 12)

A major factor in the construction of an image of the United States by the German population in the years 1945–9 was the overwhelming presence of the occupying forces in the American zone. By 1946, most of the combat troops had been replaced by 'untrained, undisciplined and unmotivated soldiery of below-average intelligence'.[2] As a result, numbers of German civilians suffered physically at the hands of belligerent, often drunken GIs, not only in Marburg where conscripts were processed, but also in several Bavarian cities. Even American women in the armed forces carried flags at night to prevent molestation. As Gimbel's exhaustive study of Marburg shows, not only were unprovoked attacks perpetrated, but watches, radios, furniture, and cameras were appropriated, personal property was looted or burned, reckless driving and road accidents were frequent occurrences, and requisitioning of accommodation was carried out with little tact or sensitivity.[3] The peace of the German countryside was regularly disturbed by hunting with spotlights and fishing with hand grenades, a modern version of frontier ways, evident also in the wearing of pistols cowboy-fashion. It is small wonder that Marburgers (and other German citizens) became disillusioned and even hostile as the uglier features of the Military Occupation were manifested.

Other aspects, however, were more welcome, more in line with what Marburgers who had a knowledge of democratic idealism expected: supplies of food, the reintroduction of public services, the provision of films, and youth activities. Generally in Germany there was a massive youth athletic programme set up as part of the work of re-education. Baseball took its place beside films and lectures as a corrective to Nazism and a guarantee against a resurgence of German nationalism.

Certainly, at the outset, the image held by Germans of those who claimed to come as conquerors and not as oppressors was an ambivalent one in which high-handed arrogance was super-imposed on regenerative goodwill. Gradually, as the role of the post-war German state (the *Bundesrepublik*) crystallized as part of America's Cold War strategy, and it was drawn as a junior partner into NATO and the Western Alliance, German attitudes, at least in political and business circles, became more homogeneous.

Even in the period immediately after the war there was something of a love affair between the victors and the defeated as, in Josef Joffe's succinct listing, 'CARE packages and capitalism, Marshall Plan aid and the Bill of Rights, free trade and federalism'[4] were all made available. It was a love affair that would endure until the time of the Vietnam War. Goods from private American agencies, ideology, and media events, which is what American aid swiftly became, were accepted willingly. As liberators with anti-Fascist slogans and as bringers of democracy, they began to win the trust of those hoping for a break with the past. The magazine *Der Ruf* (The Cry), which at its peak had a circulation of 100,000, received many contributions reflecting this attitude. With its vision of free German youth linked to 'Young Europe' it was influential upon the younger generation, but its independence, its criticism of American imperialism, and its socialist leanings – it called for the establishment of a workers' university – led to the withdrawal of its licence by the Office of Military Government United States (OMGUS) in 1947 on the grounds of 'nihilism'.

Public opinion surveys in the American, British, and French zones (such as that published by the *Frankfurter Rundschau* on 10 June 1950) revealed that the local population clearly preferred the Amis; in Berlin the favourable response was 80 per cent. Black soldiers, by dint of their sympathy for and generosity towards children, were especially popular; they were also enthusiastic fraternizers.

In the early years of the Occcupation, however, the German attitude towards the American forces was still determined by the defeated nation's own wretched situation, crisply described by Melvin Lasky: 'a ruined, poverty-stricken, brutalized people, with little to eat, everything to fear, nothing to hope for'.[5] They were subject to curfew restrictions, could not telephone or travel any distance and were vulnerable to searches, loss of property and forced labour. In so far as the Germans were without soap, the Americans appeared spick and span; in so far as they were stripped of power, the Americans appeared strong and dominant; and perhaps above all, in so far as they were hungry and destitute, the Amis, their prosperity augmented by German servants, appeared blessed with access to a steady flow of coffee, chocolate, canned food – and most coveted of all, cigarettes.[6] GIs enjoyed the highest daily calorie intake in the whole of Europe (4,200). The official allowance for Germans in the zone (1,550) was never reached. Even in the middle of 1948, Bavarian students protested with placards saying 'Even a dog needs 1,700 calories.' Children's essays, analyzed in *Neue Zeitung* (April 1948) were dominated by fantasies of food.

The docility, submissiveness, and post-totalitarian shock of the indigenous population, as recorded by observers in 1945–6, gave way to other emotions and responses, depending upon the extent and effectiveness with which American dollars were translated into food, jobs (civilian workers earned nearly $400 a month), warmth, and shelter. After the appalling winter of 1946–7, when the transport network collapsed, thousands suffered from frost-bite and angry resentment grew visibly. Early in 1947 protests against food shortages took place in Bavaria in the form of demonstrations and strikes. A year later Johannes Semler, head of the Executive Committee for Economics in the British and American zones, was dismissed for claiming that the Americans were sending only 'chicken feed' at a time when Germans were starving. He was replaced, with significant historical consequences, by Ludwig Erhard.[7] The United States did have its priorities as far as aid to Europe was concerned: Congress was loth to vote extra funds for Germany whose farmers, it suspected, were not producing as much food as they could. By the beginning of 1948, as a result of the persistence of chaos and ruin and the limited degree of substantial change, there were increasing signs of bitterness, apathy, and even fatalism in Germany. People observed that the old Weimar politicians and labour leaders were back in key positions and that ex-Nazis seemed to be better off than those who had suffered under the Third Reich.

Cabaret programmes in Frankfurt, Wiesbaden, and Kassel directed their satire at the inefficiency and corruption of German officialdom. To a lesser extent cabaret performers drew on Occupation themes including gum-chewing, food-guzzling, jazz-loving GIs, and their 'Ami-girls'. Writers and artists, however, tended to pull their punches in presenting American material for fear that the Military Government would withhold their licences. Some were sufficiently provocative to arouse official American wrath. In 1947, Munich's *Bunter Würfel* (Coloured Dice) was made to change its programme when it summed up the impact of American culture on Germany as 'cigarettes, chocolate, and penicillin'. Another show by the *Hinterlassenen* (Survivors) in Bremen was closed down for slandering the military authorities, but the troupe moved to Hamburg, where, with the blessing of the British Theatre Officer, it was free to continue its attacks on Americanization.

The physical needs of Germans were accompanied by other requirements. The phrase *die Stunde Null* (Zero Hour) implies a spiritual and cultural vacuum waiting to be filled. In the films of Wim Wenders that process has been continuously explored as the colonization of the German subconscious. Wenders has laid stress, in an interview, upon 'the German difficulties with their past'.

'One way of forgetting it . . .', he continued, 'was to accept the American imperialism.'[8] That acceptance was neither immediate nor total in the early years of the American Occupation. A 1946 report from Radio Munich by the American Chief of Section lamented, 'The staff of the station cannot avoid the impression that Bavarians would be happy if we broadcast yodelers and *Schuhplattler* [Bavarian folkdance] and *Schrammelmusik* [Viennese music for violin, guitar and accordion] twenty-four hours a day.'[9] Also, letters to the radio magazine *Hör zu*! about music broadcasts on *Nordwestdeutscher Rundfunk* complained of 'Negro music' and called for a ban on swing in favour of 'cultured' dance music. The stultification politics of the Nazis continued to resound.

The pace of Americanization was dependent less on German perceptions of American national character than on political, ideological, and industrial developments – on, for example, the Cold War and American economic penetration of Europe. The end of Axis-Allies hostility in the European theatre came on 8 May 1945. Just a few months later, in July, Henry Stimson, the retiring Secretary of War, told Lucius Clay, the American Military Commander, that the reconstruction of the German economy was essential for the creation of an atmosphere in which 'the true spirit of democracy' might be established. Whatever the degree of success achieved by American post-war propaganda, the control of resurrected media (the news agency DANA 1945, the magazines *Neue Zeitung* in 1945 and *Der Monat* in 1948, and in 1947 the establishment of thirty-two America Houses) by the Occupation forces ensured that the Germans were subjected to a flood of images and words that were, however crudely, a paradigm of democracy.

The American re-education enterprise was hampered at the outset by other imperatives of the American mission, in particular the rules on fraternization and eating in German restaurants. Self-enclosed armed service communities, 'Little Americas' in effect, had their own night-clubs, soda fountains, and commissaries, the PXs completing $80 million of business in the year 1948 when 200,000 US personnel were stationed in Germany. Ten-feet-high barbed wire fences provided what was regarded as necessary protection but they were hardly a powerful advertisement for American social ideals. In the main office building of I.G. Farben, now employed as the new United States Army

5

Headquarters, the democratic future of Germany was to be planned behind closed doors, an irony noted at the time by Walter Kolb, the city's mayor. Further anti-democratic measures were the setting up of separate facilities (toilets, streetcars) for Germans and Americans. The segregation of armed forces facilities on racial grounds also continued for several years, producing at times, in Germany and Austria, a three-way split. The widespread infractions of the regulations by lonely and bored American troops, which led swiftly to the rescinding of the original order, demonstrated the impracticality of non-fraternization (see Plate 5, between pages 82 and 83). The Army HQ in Frankfurt was an early instance of capitulation. Soon after the policy was changed in October 1945 German girls were allowed to stay overnight in men's quarters. Democracy, it seemed, was liable to oscillate between repression and licence.

To some Germans, non-fraternization was an indication of American naïveté, even stupidity, and of a lack of experience among the military. Others regarded it as further evidence of imperious tendencies. Although American troops had been welcomed with signs proclaiming 'Democracy for ever', the words *Demokratie* and *Diktatur* were merged to articulate the contradiction: *Demokratur*. Evidence of the inappropriately authoritarian nature of the 'democratization' of Germany was to be found in numerous areas of everyday living:

> It wasn't enough that the Germans should read reasonable
> editorials instead of Goebbels' propaganda, they had to read
> it at the same place in the paper as readers in New York or
> Los Angeles. It wasn't enough that policemen in Frankfurt
> were to refrain from Nazi brutalities, they also had to look
> like Texans.[10]

'Democracy', like other concepts and abstractions, remained less than relevant for a population whose needs were material and urgent. Brecht's famous '*Erst kommt das fressen, dann kommt die Moral*' (First grub, then morals) was entirely apposite at this time: newsreels such as *Welt im Film* and magazine photographs with texts reveal the enthusiastic welcome given to the ships and freight cars that brought provisions and raw materials. An extract from a passage by the editors of *Radio Illustrierte Bremen*, which praises those Americans who have given freely (or from the heart), epitomizes the German attitude:

May those take an example from this open-hearted
behaviour, those who believe that the German misery can be
solved by propaganda phrases and political slogans, all too
many of whom, unfortunately for us, they are sending over
the ocean.[11]

In any case, democracy was only to be exercised within limits: it
precluded certain types of criticism, such as attacks on the
educational system, and, while weak trade unions were allowed to
exist in 1946, the genuine workers' councils which had sprung up in
factories during the previous year were unacceptable. Radicalism
was rechanneled into a form of politics that would successfully
resist socialist change, a process achieved with some ease in the
American zone where (as in the French zone) Communism had
always been weak. Most historians are agreed that post-war
German society was *not* unified in a consensus for radical reform.

Terms other than 'democracy' have been enlisted to describe the
strategies and activities of the United States in relation to other
countries, notably 'imperialism' and 'Americanization'. A consideration of the applicability of these terms reveals a crucial
dilemma which faced the American authorities: how to maintain
restrictions on German industry (pursuing the announced policies
of decartelization and denazification) and keep the economy
stable. As the OMGUS Economic Division reported to Washington in 1946, the Morgenthau plan to return Germany to a
pre-industrial order had little chance of realization. It was held
that an impotent agrarian Germany would be vulnerable to
Communism. In addition, American industrialists sought to enter
or expand within the German economy, and their paths were
smoothed by the military, many of whom had their own business
interests. Western air forces did not damage German industry
fundamentally or permanently. As for industrial plant already
owned by US companies, the factories of Ford and General
Motors had remained intact. ITT enjoyed similar good fortune,
seizing the opportunity of removing its plants from the Russian
zone, transferring them to the American zone, and, logically in
view of its earlier links with the Axis powers, roundly denouncing
Communism. Along with National Cash Register and Singer, the
company was allowed to enter Germany on special licences in
defiance of presidential orders.

Decartelization was thwarted by large American corporations seeking a strong industrial system, and although it proceeded haltingly between 1945 and 1948, economic reconstruction was already under way, accelerating in 1947 when the policy of restricting production was reversed. Indeed, US power and resources eventually decided the fate of German industry in *all* the Western zones. Part of the report that emanated from Hoover's mission to Europe in 1947 stressed the need for the inclusion in future plans of those industrialists associated with the previous regime. Denazification and ultimately decartelization were sacrificed to German re-industrialization and American expediency. The advocacy by American big business of an economy which the German people would find familiar was far from altruistic. Despite the reference to decentralization in the 1945 Potsdam Agreement, much more could have been done to transform the German economy into a system of decentralized, competitive firms and to encourage a new class of entrepreneurs untainted by monopoly capitalism and a Nazi past, had these been priorities of the occupying powers. Small wonder, then, that Kurt Schumacher, leader of the SPD, should describe the motivation of the United States as a mixture of 'misplaced reformist zeal, shrewd power politics and plain greed'.[12]

The substantial impact of the USA upon post-war Germany at many levels was not achieved in an historical vacuum. Habermas locates the origins of German mass culture in the last decades of the nineteenth century. In this century, the tradition of Americanization dates from the period of the Weimar Republic, during which a class for jazz music was started at Frankfurt's *Städtisches Konservatorium*, and from the *Amerikanismus* of the twenties in which Berlin especially, adding its own bitter, cynical tones, eagerly participated. Kreuter and Oltmann have recently provided the following important reminder of developments in the thirties: 'An Americanization from Coca-Cola-Consumption to the star cult of Hollywood actors still characterized the everyday reality of Fascism with the first break coming with the American entry into the war in 1941.'[13] Subsequently, in the forties, American jazz enabled young people in Germany to express their disaffiliation from Nazi militarism. For their part the Nazis, notably Hitler and Hess, enjoyed the improbable Teutonic westerns of Karl May with their German-American hero 'Old Shatterhand'. Goebbels admired Clarence Brown's film version of *Anna Karenina* (1935) and hoped that *Kolberg* (1945) would prove to be a German *Gone with the Wind*.

From the mid-twenties, both for Germany and Russia, the United States represented efficiency and precision, particularly in industry. It also implied trusts rather than the looser cartels, with the IG Farben chemicals trust being founded in 1925 at a time when massive American investments were being made in the German economy. Gradually Germany, with a succession of anti-Communist administrations, was being made the main economic base of the United States in Europe. Investments by American firms totalled $475 million in 1941; three corporations, ITT, General Motors, and American IG Chemical Corporation (the subsidiary of IG Farben) retained financial and industrial links with the Nazi government during the war.[14] The fact that no IG Farben plants were destroyed – indeed, some of its more sophisticated equipment came under the protection of Washington – may not be unconnected with the company's commercial relations with Standard Oil. By 1952, 523 important German enterprises were controlled by US capital, mainly in coal, metal industries, petrol, electrical goods, cars, and chemicals.

Antonio Gramsci, in his *Prison Notebooks*, called the planned production techniques introduced between the wars 'Fordism', though in Germany Ford's image was that of the entrepreneur who enabled workers to drive shiny new cars. Egon Kisch's *Paradies Amerika* (1930) was more objective in its view of American culture than the title suggested and some intellectuals became aware of the dangers of standardization and rationalization, but generally 'Amerika' conjured visions of a new age of technology and prosperity. However, in a later decade (the forties) one observer was quick to recognize the growth of cynical, technocratic attitudes in the years immediately after the Second World War, and their consequences:

> The technocratic state of mind includes today the deliberate rejection of politics and parties, ironic and sarcastic attitudes towards Nazism, denazification, democracy, anti-Fascism and concentration on finishing one's education as speedily as possible, and on a position, money and consumer goods.[15]

In the late thirties, the Nazi Labour Front operated consumer goods enterprises, such as chain stores and food-processing plants, for the benefit of its members. It cannot be claimed, however, that before the Second World War Germany was anything like a consumer society on the pattern and at the level of the United States. Between 1933 and 1939 the output of consumer goods rose by less than 50 per cent, and from 1934 onwards the stress was on the production of synthetics and armaments. Nevertheless, while the improved standard of living was not shared by all classes, reference ought to be made to the increased consumption of meat, coffee, and butter, the increased rate of house building, the displays in department-store windows, the amount of hire purchase business, and a degree of embourgeoisement through the possession of cars, radios, furniture, and kitchen appliances. Even in 1942, consumer goods production was high compared with late thirties levels and of course stocks were obtained during the war by looting occupied nations.

It has been suggested that one of the curious features of American cultural imperialism has been its lack of any conscious 'civilizing' mission and that with a few exceptions, there has been little organized effort to export the American way of life beyond the limits of the continent. Foreigners and their concerns have historically been treated with apathy and indifference by Americans. Such an approach is consistent with Daniel Bell's description of fifties culture and consciousness as the 'end of ideology'.

The tidal wave of American popular culture that has been sweeping the globe since the Second World War is therefore due, it is claimed, to supply and demand and to the logic of industrialism, technology, and modern mass society. This attractive argument ignores American nationalism and ideological motivation. It also fails to take account of that strong sense of national identity established by the Stars and Stripes (which German women made in 1945 to attach to US Army jeeps), by political beliefs, by a written constitution, by an educative 'liberal' press, by a calendar celebrating historical events, and by the mythologizing of those events through the mass media. In Nicholas Pronay's cogent statement,

> The United States was an ideological nation, the world's first and most successful one, and . . . it had an almost total conviction about its moral right to project its ideology and to impose it by every available means on others: was democracy not 'the last best hope of mankind'?[16]

Circumstances in the American zone determined that the ideological effort underlining re-education would be equally strong – hence the use of the phrase 'Mission on the Rhine'.

American cultural imperialism in Western Germany went hand in hand with the reconstruction of capitalism, the basis for the recreation of a consumer economy. This was preceded by the Hoover Report (1947), Marshall Plan aid and currency reform (Operation Bird-Dog) in 1948. The Hoover report was reprinted in Gustav Stolper's *German Realities*, which criticized decartelization and socialist tendencies while advocating the promotion of German industry and the inclusion of Germany in the Atlantic community. The arrival of the Deutschmark in 1948 magically transformed German life (seemingly overnight) and began to turn the zones occupied by the Allies into the kind of American-style consumer society which such interventions as Stolper's were calculated to encourage.

The new Deutschmark's close similarity to the American dollar (both were printed by the US Mint in Washington) had both practical and symbolic meaning. Although large areas of rubble were to remain in the cities for some time, on 20 June 1948 the world of *Stunde Null* and *Trümmer* was replaced, in prospect and before long in reality, by a new society of mass production, marketing, materialism, and (later, in the fifties) militarism. Surveys were to show that 60 per cent of the population preferred property, jobs, and the possibility of a substantial income to all the democratic freedoms. Cherished above all was economic security, the shibboleth of the post-war years.

While the 'economic miracle' was, in general, satisfying that need – some later entertained doubts, either about its permanence or about the social and spiritual cost incurred – West Germany, like other Western European nations, was being made the receptacle for Cold War propaganda through the mass media, and for American economic penetration through investment and advertising. The irresistible flow of images supplied by American mass culture included Coca-Cola, Hollywood stars, *Time* magazine, streamlined cars, and Lucky Strike cigarettes which, prior to currency reform, became the most important single measure of value and price. The point here is that the presence of these images symbolizing the USA's material wealth encouraged and reassured those who found affluence and economic boom the solutions to individual and national difficulties. In this context, the model of the American way of life, of the oldest consumer society, became dominant in one of the newest of such societies.

To many outside observers the mass culture symbols of American affluence projected an image of the United States as not only materialistic but crude, without *Kultur*.[17] From the eighteenth century onwards conservatives and radicals had regarded European civilization as superior to American culture which was considered utilitarian and vulgar. In the thirties, 'the German image of America was that of a Philistine polyglot mongrelised community descended from convicts and the unwanted dregs of other societies.'[18] The writer Carl Zuckmayer, returning from America after the war, described it as a country without traditions from which the Germans could learn nothing. Even during the Adenauer years anti-Americanism on the right was manifested as cultural criticism based on style and taste; and in addition the American preoccupation with democracy was seen as 'softness' in view of the crucial struggle with Eastern Europe. There is also a history of left-wing alienation from American mass culture, stretching from Adorno's hatred of jazz to more recent attacks (in the magazine *Konkret*) on the corruption of the language (and the environment) by Americanisms.

An examination of the evidence, however, reveals the usual German ambivalence. The journalist Hans Habe suggested in the early fifties that productions of plays by Miller, Williams, and Wilder on the German stage gave a distorted, even malevolent caricature of American life. Yet the extraordinary success of Wilder's play, *The Skin of Our Teeth* was in large measure due to its clear and optimistic message: whatever the hardships of the past, all will be well in the future. The German title was *Wir sind noch einmal davon gekommen* (*We managed to pull through again*). And not only were scarce American magazines from *Time* to *Business Week* so popular in 1946 that a black market flourished, but the most successful German magazines of the fifties were based on American models.

The Americanization of German everyday life was, as we have noted, hardly a new and sudden phenomenon. Coca-Cola, described by its president Robert Woodruff as 'the essence of American capitalism', was first established in Germany at Essen in 1929, and despite official disapproval it flourished during the thirties. Hollywood films could be seen in Germany right up to the entry of the United States into the Second World War: streamlining, which had become the American synonym for modernity in general, was used by the Third Reich 'for an aesthetic demonstration of technical superiority and for propagating the alleged modernity and progressivism of the regime'.[19] Finally, jazz in a variety of cultural roles retained for decades the popularity established through new technology during the Weimar Republic.

If Bavarian beer mugs, the furniture of 1900, and the art of the Third Reich demonstrate the fallibility of German taste, the reverence for *Kultur* and the characteristic known as *Bildungsbeflissenheit* (eagerness to be educated) must also be acknowledged. Furthermore, the practice of German writers making a firm distinction between *Literatur* and *Unterhaltungsliteratur* (entertainment) provides a suitable analogy for the separation of *Kultur* and mass culture. Yet the two could come together in semiotically intriguing combinations: Alfred Kazin, the literary critic, witnessed a young Austrian playing boogie-woogie for bored, coke-drinking US soldiers in Salzburg. On the wall were drawings of Mozart, Schubert, Richard Strauss, and Beethoven. During that year, 1948, the last named composer is mentioned in a mildly nationalistic hit entitled *Trizonesien-Song*. Although the 'old time' is now a thing of the past, classic figures are evoked to support the claim that the inhabitants of the tri-zone possess humour, intellect, and *Kultur*: 'Goethe himself comes from the Trizone/ Beethoven's birthplace is well-known/ And you cannot say that about China.' Also in 1948, an issue of *Radio Illustrierte Bremen*, in its photo section 'Bühne + Mode', juxtaposes pictures of performances of *Cosi Fan Tutte* and Schiller's *Braut von Messina* with a shot of a customer in Stuttgart buying a pullover on which are picked out the names of five leading brands of American cigarette.

At the end of the war, German perceptions of themselves, of Americans, and of their respective countries varied enormously. The spectrum of German opinion ran from unreconstructed Nazis and those nostalgic for Prussian authoritarianism, through pro-American capitalists, to decentralists, socialists, and Communists. Individuals with a high socio-economic status were consistently pro-American, as were the inhabitants of West Berlin where the children enthusiastically welcomed the 'raisin-bombers' during the 1948–9 airlift. (The blockade of Berlin cannot be underestimated for it altered American attitudes towards a vulnerable citizenry who had 'chosen' the USA and, as news of airlift deliveries saturated the West German media, changed German attitudes towards Americans as well.) A 1947 study of over two thousand people, mainly in Baden-Württemberg and Bavaria, revealed that 'no fewer than seven in ten persons were favourably disposed towards the US in the issue of national capitalism'.[20] At the same time, most West Germans interviewed on the subject in the same year thought National Socialism a good idea badly carried out. Naturally the US Occupation stifled any resurgence of power which surviving Nazis might have anticipated.

The confusions and contradictions of post-war Germany under Allied control render it difficult to grasp by means of historical details and the imagination. Many people are still reluctant to discuss the period and for the researcher it seems to disintegrate into an untidy jumble of contemporary reports and anecdotes. They may be the heart of the matter. One definition asserts: 'History is made up of wisps of narrative . . . the people do not exist as a subject but as a means of millions of insignificant and serious little stories.'[21] At least the images of the late forties retain a mixture of the evocative and the opaque. They include an American soldier prising away a street sign which reads *Adolf-Hitler Strasse*; Berlin children with bricks, flags (American and British), and a toy plane playing *Luftbrücke* (Airlift); the black singer Al Edwards in US Army uniform performing for AFN (Armed Forces Network) in a beer cellar under a sign in Gothic script which translates as 'Who is sick must live healthily'; and the increasingly affluent lifestyle of the bourgeoisie represented by *Der Spiegel*'s photographs and advertisements.

The period of the Occupation, one marked by economic colonization, cultural imperialism, and the re-education programme, was the prologue to a more developed Americanization. Chewing gum and Lucky Strike, whose packaging alone symbolized the beautiful new world of modernity, were the harbingers of McDonalds, corporation skyscrapers, and nuclear missiles.[22] The new 'soft' cultural nationalism of the early eighties which has appeared notably but not exclusively among the young and the left in West Germany is a reaction against the hegemonic intrusion of 'Yankee' images, technology, and fashions. To the visitor this kind of intrusion has had the effect of pushing the German past into museums and behind the walls of sixteenth-century towns like Rothenburg ob der Tauber. Commentators play down the anti-Americanism represented by this resurgent patriotism because in a 1982 poll, 75 per cent of West Germans expressed a favourable view of the USA. However, the acceptance of the American presence since 1945 has never been total, and the rejection of ideology was a constant feature of West German intellectual life until the 1960s. With historical imagination we can hear, mingled with the calls for 'cultural regression' and 'de-Westernization', the voices of schoolchildren at a post-war cinema greeting the opening of *Welt im Film* with the Allies' marching orders: '*Haut sie raus, den Tommy, haut sie raus, den Ami, . . .*'

Chapter two

Re-education: 'Your Job in Germany'

In 1948, Richard Alexander, chief of the Education and Religious Affairs branch of the Military Government, wrote:

> The great mass of Germans has learned nothing from the war as yet, and, the more readily they acquire economic security, the more certain they are to take the same pattern as before. It is ridiculous to think that in three years' time we can make over the thinking of a nation that is so badly infected with arrogant nationalism as Germany was.[1]

Alexander's views were not those of an isolated individual. In several quarters there appears to have been some reluctance to sustain American informational and educational agencies with international responsibilities once the war was over. The Voice of America almost faded into insignificance between 1945 and 1947, while the Office of War Information, peopled by New Dealers whom Congress distrusted, was abolished outright. Further inhibiting factors were the belief, articulated by Secretary of State James Byrnes in Stuttgart on 6 September 1946, that the USA should in due course encourage the Germans to run their own affairs, and the paradox of an open, democratic society forcing its political values upon others. Not, it might be added, that the democratic features of the USA were the most prominent during the late 1940s when paranoid anti-Communism was widespread.

Nevertheless, President Truman and others were aware of the need to explain democracy to the liberated and defeated countries. In the case of Germany, re-education was undertaken less with a view to remould the German consciousness than with the wish to prevent a recurrence of aggression. Increasingly the motive became the American desire to integrate Germany into an anti-Soviet West European coalition. Although the promotion of democracy as the American way of life was retained, from the beginning of 1947 the original goal of democratization took second place to the imperatives of anti-Communism.

Whatever the impetus, re-education was a continuation of earlier activities such as Voice of America broadcasts in 1944 which provided information about industry, geography, songs, beliefs, and individual American states. Prisoners of war such as Walter Hallstein, later Secretary of State in the Ministry of Foreign Affairs, were at that time already studying American ideas and institutions in such camps as Fort Benning. The curriculum included politics (the New Deal), agriculture, the history of the USA, and the nature of democracy. Feature films were shown but in addition prisoners were obliged to watch Frank Capra's celebrated documentary films, *Why We Fight*, conceived as training films for Allied troops. The last of the seven fifty-minute films *War Comes to America*, is, in isolation, serviceable as a re-education document. After a visual history of the USA, it examines the way Americans have reacted to the war and have committed themselves to the defence of freedom and democracy. The series was also shown in the first months of the Occupation at American Embassies in Germany and Japan.

For the inculcation of democratic ideas in Germany after 1945, the school was central, and the US Educational Mission to Germany proposed the setting up of an American-style comprehensive system in its 1946 report. Later, in 1948, the *Saturday Evening Post* was proposing its own version of democratization, one in which the reference to 'our friends' implies the ideal of Germany as an ally; six years later West Germany was admitted to NATO: 'We should establish institutes in the American zone, staffed with Americans, where German teachers could find a new outlook, a new hope. Each of these German teachers, once they are *our friends*, would influence many German children (my emphasis).'[2] Proposals such as these came to naught. Internal divisions, provocative behaviour, and poor judgement, along with stiff resistance from the Germans who clung to the values of antiquity, Christianity, and elitism, ensured that German education at the secondary level retained its traditional structure.

Americanization of young Germans was much more successful outside the schools, resulting in an admiration for all things 'made in the USA': in the late forties, young people would visit America Houses twice as frequently as the generation of their parents. During what came to be known as the chocolate candy era, the enthusiasm for proselytizing German youth was indicated by the investment of DM60 million. At Youth Centers councils and mini-parliaments were organized, newspapers were read and discussed, and magazines which were to gain a wide circulation were planned. The titles – *Junge Welt* (Young World), *Ins Neue Leben* (Into the New Life), *Die Zukunft* (The Future) – have an optimistic, 'New World' flavour. GIs played a major part in some of these activities, in particular helping Germans, whom they treated just like American kids, to form jazz bands and sports teams. A young German's proudest boast was, 'I know a GI personally. He says I speak English like a Yank.'

The universities, however, have been more hostile towards change than almost any other social institution in modern Germany. When they reopened in 1946–7, their elderly professoriate, abetted by officials at the Ministry of Education, was quite satisfied to recreate the conditions obtaining before 1933. Unpersuaded by the argument that democracy needed strengthening at every point, they even acquiesced in anti-democratic behaviour. It was discovered in July 1946 that professors at Erlangen University were attacking democratic ideas and expounding the virtues of National Socialism. Even in the spring of 1948 the *Saturday Evening Post* was denouncing the 'scandalous' conditions in Germany's nationalistic universities. The effective neutralization of such activities was hampered by a lack not just of money but of essential books and periodicals as well. It took a report in *Newsweek* and the realization that Russia was winning the Cold War propaganda battle to release $4 million, which was used to buy paper for textbooks. Meanwhile, private institutions attempted to improve matters so that Würzburg University, for example, received a substantial gift of books from the Smithsonian.

Nevertheless, as early as November 1946 it was reported that lecturers and officials as well as students were eager to welcome as many academic visitors as the USA could send. With the exception of a visit to Frankfurt for a semester by faculty from the University of Chicago, the traffic tended to be in the other direction. The same was true for students: no American students were allowed to visit Germany on an exchange programme until April 1948, in which year 214 German students were sent to the United States. Inevitably, exchanges encouraged a stronger commitment to democratic principles, but a more general commitment – to internationalism – was often the result. The more independent spirits among young German visitors were critical of American universities where they encountered too much emphasis on technical expertise, a system where undergraduates were indulged and counselled into a state of dependency and, in some cases, anti-intellectualism.

In German universities American Studies was introduced after the Second World War with the hope 'that they might contribute both to Germany's political and scholarly rebirth and to that reform of its education which was felt to be indispensable to its democratic future.'[3] Such expectations were rarely fulfilled. In 1948 American aid was instrumental in the relocation of part of what is now called Humboldt University, East Berlin as the Free University of Berlin (in the western part of the city). From the very beginning American Studies courses proliferated and visiting professors from the US supplemented the local teaching staff. To some extent, students were brought into the decision-making process, but concessions of this kind were gradually eroded. In other universities, from about 1947 and when American money was available, American Studies was introduced as a specialization within the traditional framework. Certainly, in the post-war decade, such courses found their way into a majority of universities and American Literature achieved a special status.

However the interest of a particular professor was often crucial. In the 1948–9 session, American Studies was ranked only fifteenth on a list of Area Studies in German universities, and by 1958, 'American' teaching was still largely a luxury for German academics. An inter-departmental *Amerika-Institut* was initiated in Frankfurt in 1946, but American Studies was seen as a forum for co-operative work rather than as a separate discipline. A similar institute was inaugurated in 1949 in Munich, one which in its early years was run largely by Americans. Ironically in the fifties there was more 'Americanist' activity in those areas which had been under British or French occupation.

One of the more prominent agencies of democratic re-education was the *Amerika-Haus*. The name America House – they were also known as US Information Centers (USIC) – emerged as a result of asking German users of American libraries to suggest a name acknowledging US endeavours to inform the indigenous population. Those endeavours were interpreted as opening a 'window to the West' – hence the name, America House. It was first employed in October 1947 in a Military Government report describing the purpose of the centres, though the two small libraries, at Bad Homburg and Marburg, which marked the beginning of these institutions, were opened somewhat earlier. About 700 well-used educational and reference books from surplus army stock comprised the content of the Bad Homburg library when, under the auspices of the Psychological Warfare Division of the Supreme Headquarters Allied Expeditionary Force (SHAEF), it started to operate in July 1945. The volumes were kept in a reading-room where they were accessible to a restricted number of German civilians. Later this library formed the basis of the Wiesbaden America House which was opened in 1947. Already, in November 1946, there were sixteen US Information Centers in the American zone. In its heyday, 1949–50, when attendance throughout Germany was over one million a month, USIC programmes were being run in 27 completed America Houses and 136 affiliated Reading-Rooms in smaller towns. The US High Commissioner, John L. McCloy, opening the Hanover America House in May 1950, described the institution unequivocally as 'a House of Freedom'. By that time the role of the America House as a purveyor of democratic ideas had clearly intensified and it was assuming different meanings for its opponents. To the nationalists on the Right it was a reminder of the humiliation of the Occupation; to the supporters of the Left it was an example of the reviled 'cultural imperialism' of the United States. Such considerations were alien to small groups of vagabonds, refugees, and the homeless who embraced the well-heated rooms and comfortable chairs.

In 1947 the year after its establishment, the Stuttgart House started a press information archive to assist local journalists, but in general the library, the embryo of the America House, has stayed at the centre of the institution's work providing on average 16,000 books, about a quarter of them in German, and taking books to the population through mobile libraries. Even at the end of the war their supply of American newspapers and periodicals went some way towards satisfying the considerable interest in whatever reflected the American way of life. In addition, the libraries, which possessed holdings of gramophone records and music scores, soon developed a programme of lectures, films, and cultural activities. At the *Amerika-Haus* in Heidelberg American experts gave talks four times a week and in May 1947, an exhibition, 'Projecting America', was mounted. Similar displays – 'Architecture in the USA', 'American Journalism', 'American Folklore', 'Political Democracy in the United States and in England', and 'TVA: Tennessee Valley Authority'– followed, using the visual techniques of photographs, scale models, plans, and texts to reveal aspects of American life. Exhibitions of paintings and sculpture as well as concerts went some way to countering accusations of philistinism.

Some indication of the change of role experienced at the America Houses is given by different reports on Military Government Regulations. The first entitled 'Re-education and Reorientation', states in December 1945: 'Information Control will provide the Germans with information which will influence them to understand and accept the United States programme of occupation, and to establish for themselves a stable, peaceful, and acceptable government.' By September 1947, with broader foreign policy objectives in mind, the term 're-education' had been dropped from a similar report which now proclaimed that, while furthering the 'democratic reorientation of Germany', Information Control would 'foster the assimilation of the German people into the society of peaceful nations through the revival of international cultural relations'.[4]

Under the re-education programme, 'democracy' had been an ideological counter to Nazism. With relations between Russia and the United States deteriorating in 1947, the year of the Truman Doctrine and of 'Operation Talkback', American and British political beliefs were paraded with more and more vigour as alternatives to the Communism practised in Russia. An OMGUS report from this period refers to the attacks against the USA emanating from Russian-controlled media in Germany and announces an informational programme to emphasize that 'a democratic system, in contrast to the operation of a police state, safeguards the individual's rights and dignity'.[5] Very quickly, the Information Center became less a purely educational agency than an instrument of the Military Government in the battle of ideas: it assisted, for instance, in the distribution of more than four million anti-Communist brochures throughout Germany. In the course of the next year, 1948, the shift of emphasis in USIC programmes and in the libraries became evident. Notable additions to the shelves were Victor Kravchenko's *I Chose Freedom*, and *Slave Labor in Soviet Russia* by David Dallin and Boris Nicolaevsky.

In 1947, then, following the emergency of 'Operation Talkback', the America Houses in existence were brought under more rigid ideological control (although the efforts to make Germans more aware of their facilities did not show results until well into 1948). A decision was also made in October to add seven USICs to the twenty already operating. Hamburg was chosen as the site of the first American library to be established outside the American zone. It came under the control of the American General Consulate and formed the nucleus of the *Amerika-Haus* created in 1950. In the same year, a special programme including books, newspapers, newsreels, and documentaries was set up at Berlin USIC to attract visitors from the Eastern zone. More than 100,000 people were attracted to the film performances during the first year. Meanwhile, the programme of lectures and discussions for German groups and institutions experienced no diminution. Not only were purely American topics such as 'The US Constitution' and 'Black Culture in the US' dealt with, but comparisons were made between aspects of Germany and America – for example, political parties or the administration of justice. These activities were supported by bibliographies referring to books in the USIC libraries that were made available to German firms and schools. Sometimes, books on a particular theme were given as a permanent loan to works libraries or to schools whence came the teachers who, along with professors, students, writers, and journalists, constituted the most avid users of the resources of the America Houses.

The officers and officials of the Military Government were often directly involved in the lecturing programme, especially for such topics as American democracy, or the meaning of Western civilization. An American Speakers Bureau was set up to provide qualified lecturers for German audiences, and increasingly American guest professors lectured in the USICs, supplemented by 'consultants' from the State or War Departments. One evening a week was given over to cultural activities: a concert of modern American music, perhaps, or a discussion of cultural life in the US. German-American groups would also gather at an America House or at a private American home for a joint reading of an American play.

An example of the kind of visitor the USICs liked to promote is the composer Paul Hindemith. A German who had spent the war years in the United States, Hindemith paid a visit in 1947 to Frankfurt, practically his home town, where he reported to old friends and others on his 1946 composition, 'A Requiem (for those we love)', based upon Walt Whitman's great American Civil War poem, 'When Lilacs Last in the Dooryard Bloom'd'. Hindemith had observed how, following the death of President Roosevelt, the passage of his coffin through the American nation stirred up the same feelings of respect and grief as had Abraham Lincoln's casket in the nineteenth century. It was for its description of Lincoln's posthumous journey as well as for the democratic sentiments he found there that Hindemith chose the Whitman poem. In his requiem, he sought to make a musical offering of a 'song of freedom' to those on both sides killed in the Second World War and to express America's vital democracy as a model for international harmony.

Not surprisingly, in the light of his strong democratic beliefs, Hindemith was invited in late 1948 to tour the American zone and, as conductor, lecturer, and general cultural ambassador, to assist in the reorientation programme. This was the year which saw the European premiere of his requiem in Vienna; the German premiere, in Berlin, did not take place until the late fifties. Hindemith's tour took him to various urban centres in Germany: at the America House, Munich he lectured on 'The Musical Ethos', while at Darmstadt and Wiesbaden he spoke on 'Music in the USA'. Hindemith's visit early in 1949 was not accomplished without some controversy. Except in Berlin, then a beleaguered city, his frequent assertions of allegiance to the USA were received coolly by students and musicians, some of whom felt Hindemith owed a debt to his native country where he had been trained.

One aspect of American policy in the late forties was the encouragement of Germans to run their own national affairs, albeit as a client state. This was reflected in the microcosm of the

USIC, where most of the local administration was, in any case, done by Germans (who increasingly were given experience in the US). In Heidelberg in 1949, German officials, over a period of a fortnight, engaged in a discussion of political problems and possible solutions with members of the town's citizenry. In addition, as the election for the Bundestag approached, lectures and seminars were arranged to help voters understand the electoral system and the campaign issues. Further still, as the period of total occupation came to an end, efforts were made to provide more information at USICs about European history and culture, so equipping the Germans for re-entry to the international comity of states.

Up to that point, the efforts of the America Houses to reduce the degree of Americanization were limited by their role as overt agents of a military regime shaped by the Cold War and its accompanying attitudes. Indeed, an acceptance of the proselytizing process was evident in letters protesting against the curtailment of the USIC programme early in 1951. Correspondents fearful of 'the fire which the Communist Power is trying to start here' insisted that military superiority needed to be complemented by 'sufficient moral resistance', the strengthening of which would need the efforts of the America House.[6]

One of the more important areas of America House work was the assembling of film libraries for showing documentary films; in this way the authorities were able to attract half a million people monthly. The importance of film as information and influence had been recognized in the USA during the thirties. Subsequently in the Second World War documentaries were seen to be particularly suited for both enacting propaganda and for criticizing its use by the enemy – in such films as *Paradies Amerika*, for example, which portrayed the US as a country where crime, vice, and poverty were the principal characteristics.

Government involvement in documentary film-making was vastly expanded and the development of the genre became the province of the Office of War Information (OWI), whose New Deal ideology was evident in the films they selected and/or made. With the declared aim of the political, social, and economic reorientation of Germany, American documentaries dubbed into German were shown – at first separately, later accompanied by feature films and the newsreel *Welt in Film* – from the very beginning of the post-war period.[7] The use of sites other than movie cinemas and America Houses, such places as town halls, schools, even the outdoors, ensured that the films reached a larger, more varied audience, including the less well educated who were considered more impressionable. But for the Military Government film programme, many people in rural areas would have been deprived of motion pictures altogether, even in 1951.

Generally, during the early stages of the Occupation, the films shown (having been approved for Germany in the OWI *Operational Plan for Germany*, February 1945) belonged to easily defined categories – documentaries illustrating the war and interpreting it ideologically (*Fighting Lady*, *Why We Fight*, *Tarawa*, *Autobiography of a Jeep*) or 'American Scene' documentaries (*The Town*, *Cowboy*, *Steeltown*, *TVA*). The last mentioned, *TVA* (Tennessee Valley Authority), was a multi-layered work. Its central theme of land reclamation harked back to the thirties, but its democratic message urging the individual to co-operate with others in the community was timeless. In addition its depiction of natural destruction remedied by experts ('new pioneers') implied a future in which a better society would be created through science, education, and the exercise of reason. Also available but not mentioned in *The Operational Plan*, were a number of commercially sponsored shorts on industrial, scientific, and agricultural subjects, acquired and distributed by the International Motion Pictures branch of the State Department.

The Operational Plan for Germany went on to advise that future documentaries should, if produced by OWI, project America's image and relate the history of the war, or otherwise should stress Germany's responsibility for starting the war and for the holocaust which ensued. An ICD (International Control Division) officer would state that the main effort of the division was to indict Germany for its war crimes, while the film director Billy Wilder (see the essay on *A Foreign Affair*) later recalled that, for their ration cards to be accepted, Germans needed a stamp certifying that they had seen films of Nazi atrocities.

At the end of the war the successful documentary teams were broken up, the better known figures such as John Huston, William Wyler, and Frank Capra returned to Hollywood and government support dwindled. Attempts to get a documentary movement started ran up against bureaucracy and the reluctance of Congress to fund a solid, well-organized programme. Nevertheless, a documentary film unit was created in Berlin in 1947 as part of the reorientation plan and by 1950 an appreciable number of short films had been made for exhibition in German cinemas. Indeed, Stuart Schulberg, the Head of the Documentary Unit, hoped to encourage German film-makers to abandon their excessive commitment to aesthetics, to be more responsive to objectivity, and so develop an indigenous documentary film industry.

Apart from *Es liegt an Dir* (It's Up to You) which, by tracing German history from 1919 to 1948, showed a potentially decent people overwhelmed by the instinct for evil also present in the German mentality, two themes were dominant in the work of the unit. Both themes (interlinked) arose from national and international circumstances: the recovery of the German economy and the Cold War. *Step by Step* (1949) showed the rebuilding of Berlin's largest printing plant, while *Made in Germany* (1949–50) begins and ends with images of a modern consumer society. The brightly lit, well-stocked windows and neon advertisements of 1929 provide a foretaste of currency reform, kitchen equipment, and leather goods in the late forties. In between 'Germany began to *misuse* (my emphasis) her economy' for propaganda and war. Now, with the Marshall Plan providing the raw materials for German industry to manufacture and export, and with the new Deutschmark providing a financial incentive, 'West Germany could really get down to business' (*sic*). More directly ideological were films about Berlin: *Between East and West* (1949) related the story of the city from the end of the war up to and including the crisis period of the blockade, while *The Bridge* (1948–9) used an American pilot and a member of the German unloading crew at Tempelhof to create, through their sentimental friendship, a consensual, unitary perspective on the Berlin airlift. The most interesting and revealing of these films is *Two Cities* (1949), a comparison between Stuttgart and Dresden, contrasting the drabness of the latter with the affluence of the US zone city. *Two Cities* conveniently refuses to acknowledge its Cold War bias. There are no political posters in Stuttgart, it is claimed, but Greta Garbo stars in *Ninotchka* at the local movie palace. It is a city without propaganda, intones the pious voice-over while the screen fills with images of glistening kitchenware, lengths of expensive suiting, and the latest shoe fashions in high street windows.

With such examples it comes as little surprise to learn that in 1949 the US Advisory Commission on Information listed as the main criticism of documentaries in Europe the blatant nature of their propaganda. The lesson was wilfully ignored. In 1952 the US Information Service sent some Hollywood writers and producers to Germany in order to make films about the 'Communist menace'. One result, *Streetcar Called Freedom*, was a naïve fantasy about a streetcar which, by running loose in East Berlin, leaves a panorama of dingy streets for the glitter and freedom of West Berlin's commodity cornucopia. When the film was previewed in Hamburg, a student left half-way through, uttering but one word: Thick!

Re-education failed for a variety of reasons: poverty of resources; the initial emphasis (made in the documentary film *Your Job in Germany*, for example) on conquest and collective German guilt, responsible in part for German resistance; the shift from fear of Fascism to fear of Communism; and, above all, the irony of a military government as a model of and symbol of democracy. Edward Petersen has phrased this tellingly: 'Generals can scarcely command a society to be more democratic', and he added a further reason: 'Most Americans were poorly trained ideologically. They knew democracy was the best system, that it had something to do with freedom, with being tolerant and peace-loving, but that was about as far as ideological discussion usually could go.'[8]

However, if all OMGUS sought by 1948 was the reconstruction of the German economy and a Cold War status quo, the Occupation (and its Americanization potential) succeeded best when it stopped trying. Ideological reproduction and transfer were then allowed to take place as a consequence of the free market economy, and the unrestricted operation of American business and the mass media. It was American goods which were to be the revolutionary missionaries for the American way of life.

Chapter three

Film: The Affair of Billy Wilder's *A Foreign Affair*

William Fox (of 20th Century Fox) claimed that American trade followed American movies rather than the American flag. In the twenties such films, celebrating the ideals of consumption, were notably successful in promoting American products abroad, especially automobiles. They were the source of images and fantasies about the New World that were embraced by Europeans including German artists, intellectuals, and white-collar workers. Weimar's ideas of fashion, style, leisure, and entertainment – in short, what was defined as 'modern' – were dominated by American mass culture.

After the Second World War, Hollywood films were seen to be influential in pushing Germans (and, in a more consciously interventionist manner in 1948, Italians) along what one reporter, Allan Chellas, has called 'the bumpy road to democracy'. Genre films (musicals and westerns, for example) portrayed the ideology of US culture as stable, invariable; contradictions and conflicts are exposed but their resolution repeatedly affirms the ideals of 'Americanization'. Movies with contemporary settings functioned as information and advertisements depicting the components (radios, cars, refrigerators, telephones, bathtubs) of a high standard of living based on materialism.

In Germany, however, the indoctrination path was for a time decidedly bumpy as a result of poor communication and co-operation between the American film industry and the Military Government. Revenue from the exhibition of Hollywood films was accumulated in accounts held in Germany. These Reichsmarks could not be changed into dollars and could be used for only a limited number of purposes in the zones. Consequently the

American studios restricted the number of films for Germany in order to put pressure on the military authorities. This served to exacerbate a situation where the supply of films was already limited and prints were scarce. Up to mid-1946 only forty-three feature films had been released and by mid-1948 only another thirty-nine.[1]

By 1950 observers reported that many Germans had never heard of *The Best Years of Our Lives*, *Mr Smith Goes to Washington*, *The Snake Pit*, *The Oxbow Incident*, *Crossfire*, or *Intruder in the Dust*. Dealing as these films did with post-war problems, political corruption, insanity, vigilantes, anti-semitism, and racism, it was feared that they could be used as anti-American propaganda. Hitchcock's disturbing *Shadow of a Doubt* slipped through the net, presumably as a result of its small-town setting and its Thornton Wilder script, while *The Best Years Of Our Lives* was reviewed in Germany in 1948. Movies not approved might still receive distribution but the earnings were blocked.

A 1949 survey showed that less than a quarter of German movie-goers in the American zone thought the best American films were being made available to them. Conservative elements for their part frowned on the 'decadence' of frivolous musicals and on the 'impertinence' of mentioning Gershwin (in *Rhapsody in Blue*) along with Beethoven and Schubert. To those in the industry, and in the OWI, the issue was less one of quality than of entertainment value, a preference not solely based on the profit motive. Audiences were liable to resist the propaganda that was pervasive in documentaries and newsreels in the early years of the Occupation while welcoming entertainment and absorbing it as ideology. Darryl F. Zanuck, addressing the Writers' Congress in Los Angeles in 1943, advised his audience, 'If you have something worthwhile to say, dress it in the glittering robes of entertainment and you will find a ready market . . .', adding 'without entertainment no propaganda film is worth a dime'.[2]

It might seem unusual to find such sentiments echoed by the director Billy Wilder in a memorandum (appended to this chapter) for the Film, Theater and Music Branch of the Information Control Division, written in August 1945.[3] As the creator of cynical, witty, and sophisticated movies, Wilder appears to be an unlikely source of apologetics for either Americanism or escapism. However, for a brief period in the summer of 1945, probably a few weeks in August, Wilder served as a Military Government Film Officer in Berlin where he was employed to make recommendations on the reorganization and denazification of the German film industry.

In that year, 1945, Wilder's *The Lost Weekend* (Paramount) had appeared and provided one of the climaxes of his career, winning Academy Awards for best picture, direction, and screenplay. Born in Austria, Wilder had started out as a journalist in Vienna before working on screenplays in Germany. With the rise of Hitler, he fled the country arriving in the United States (via Mexico) in 1933. After teaming up, in 1937, with Charles Brackett to write screenplays, Wilder began to enjoy some success in Hollywood. His first directorial contribution to the war effort, *Five Graves to Cairo* (Paramount, 1943), was quickly followed by the equally successful *Double Indemnity* (Paramount, 1944), now seen as a classic *film noir*.

Like the Office of War Information in formulating its *Operational Plan for Germany* – referred to below – Wilder, for different reasons, was aware of the consistently high level of technical quality needed in entertainment films if they could be expected to emulate the impact and influence of a movie such as the admirable – by Wilder's criteria – *Mrs Miniver* (1942). Earlier in the memo he casts an approving glance at *Cover Girl* (1944) simply because it is a love story, contains music, and is made in technicolor. This can be considered as Wilder's version of Zanuck's 'glittering robes of entertainment': the emphasis is firmly on production values which he regards as a prerequisite for propaganda.

The rest of Wilder's memorandum contains, along with comments on aspects of post-war Germany, brief references to the theme and story of Wilder's proposed 'German' film. Wilder begins with the straightforward tale of a GI in the Occupation forces and a local girl, but the girl quickly becomes a German woman whose husband has been killed in an air-battle. Wilder's narrative would not, however, be sentimental; it would conclude with the soldier returning to the United States, the girl remaining in Germany but not without hope for the future. So far, the skeletal scenario sounds untypical of Wilder's work, despite the absence of a happy ending, and closer to conventional Hollywood 'entertainment', but the director also announces that he wishes to 'touch on fraternization, on homesickness, on black market'.

Thus, the atmosphere, if not the plot of *A Foreign Affair* (Paramount, 1948) is in the first stages of construction.[4]

The process is one of ideas and plans gradually emerging from Wilder's personal experiences and his conversations with people in the 'mad, depraved, starving' city of Berlin whose loquacious, insolent inhabitants Wilder has habitually regarded with a mixture of admiration and dislike. Those people range here from German academics and General Gavin (possibly the model for Plummer, the forceful but compassionate colonel in *A Foreign Affair* played by Millard Mitchell) to taxi-drivers and cheap whores in the Femina-Bar. Wilder's trips to the black market under the Reichstag, his investigations of American army slang, his frequent photographic excursions – all testify to his desire for authenticity.

Wilder's affection for Berlin has been evident since 1929 in the screenplay (his first) for *Menschen Am Sonntag*, directed by Robert Siodmak. Much of *A Foreign Affair* was shot in the ruins of Berlin, described by one of the Congressmen in the film as looking like 'chicken innards at fryin' time'. Colonel Plummer takes the Congressional delegation – and the audience – on a tour of the devastated city, taking in the Reichschancellery where Hitler married and later died with Eva Braun, the Adlon Hotel, the Unter den Linden, and the Tiergarten. Wilder also brought back from Berlin such items as street-signs, posters, and even doorbells for later shooting in the studio. Brackett's own German-made grand piano was used in the night-club scenes. Such authenticity elicited comparisons with the contemporaneous Italian movement of neo-realism. Rossellini's *Germany, Year Zero*, with its bleak documentary treatment of bomb-damaged streets, queues for food, and black market deals, was made in 1947. *Le Nouvel Observateur*'s review of *A Foreign Affair* carried the headline: 'C'est Rossellini en version ironique.'

While the *Government Manual for the Motion Picture Industry* (1942), with its headings 'Yardsticks for War Pictures', 'The Home Front', 'The Fighting Forces', envisaged a general American audience, *The Operational Plan for Germany* (1945)[5] was aimed at opinion-makers in the US and eventually Germany.[6] However, the underlying values were the same. The former advised that the war be depicted as a democratic enterprise geared to Roosevelt's Four Freedoms; the latter selected particular feature films in order to promote democracy and traditional American principles. Consequently *Gone with the Wind* (MGM, 1939) and *The Grapes of*

Wrath (20th Century Fox, 1940), both of which are now seen as responses to the Depression of the thirties, were rejected as insufficiently positive in their portrayal of American life. On the other hand *The Seventh Cross* (MGM, 1944), a movie about anti-Fascists within Germany itself, was banned for fear it might encourage resistance to the Occupation troops. Thus, the victors identified with their ex-enemies!

Although *The Operational Plan* allowed that 'a picture showing that America too has its troubles and problems may very well be included', such a work could only be shown if it also presented attempts to deal with these problems;[7] and in 1948 this chauvinism was encouraged by a strong financial incentive. American film companies were permitted to convert foreign currency (i.e. Deutschmarks) into dollars at attractive rates provided the best elements of American life were reflected. The number of films released rose from sixty-four (in the 1948–9 period) to 145 (1949–50). Re-education imperatives and the American film industry's profit motive ensured that permitted Hollywood movies became standard fare for the post-war generation of Germans in the American zone, and that, after a brief flowering of neo-realist film-making in East Berlin and Hamburg, a weak, splintered West German film industry would be dominated by American economic interest, which was not the intention of the Military Government. General McClure saw at first hand how Hollywood sought 'to establish an exclusive position for American films and American distribution machinery'.[8]

A Foreign Affair certainly addressed particular 'troubles and problems'. As reports in the *New York Times* reveal, domestic impressions of Germany focused upon the Nazi past, the black market, and alluring women. In the film, Colonel Plummer articulates these worries: 'Seems back home they've got an idea this here is one big picnic and all we do is swing in hammocks with blond frauleins, swap cigarettes for castles in the Rhine and soak our feet in sparkling Moselle.' He even accepts some of the criticisms: 'Maybe some of you PX millionaires have found out that you can parlay a pack of cigarettes into something more than twenty smokes. After all, this isn't a boy scout camp.'

The extremes of American avarice, arrogance, and contempt were not displayed but Wilder's residence in Germany had taught him, long before making the film, that the American GI was 'no flag-waving hero or a theorizing apostle of democracy.'[9] Some GIs were so nostalgic for home and the 'American way of life' (the blueberry pie and chocolate milk shakes of small-town mythology), they had no desire ever to see a foreign country again. Others, indifferent to the suffering in Germany's ruins, seemed determined to exhibit only 'empty materialism and spiritual poverty', as diplomat George Kennan phrased it. So the Occupation troops, like many characters in Wilder's films, are presented as opportunists on the look-out for a fast buck. In the process, re-education is passed over in favour of exploiting Berliners who also use guile for self-preservation. However, the Berlin airlift of 1948–9 made a more positive view of Berliners both possible and necessary, putting into question Wilder's cynicism.

A *Foreign Affair* was provocative in a variety of ways. Mike, a US Army corporal, dismisses Congress as 'a bunch of salesmen that's got their foot in the right door', and the tone of the film gave a sceptical impression of Congressional fact-finding junkets to Europe. Wilder's view of GIs as materialistic colonizers of a city-wide slum, his exposure of a ubiquitous black market condoned and utilized by military personnel, and his relatively favourable depiction of the night-club performer with Nazi connections played by Marlene Dietrich, only made matters worse.

An indignant attack on the film was delivered from the floor of Congress obliging the Department of Defense to issue a statement to the effect that *A Foreign Affair* gave a false picture of a decent and honourable army of occupation.[10] It should, of course, be noted that HUAC's first set of Hollywood hearings in the previous year had, in effect, challenged the film industry to demonstrate its patriotism. Later, in the *Quarterly of Film, Radio and TV* (1952–3), Stuart Schulberg, who had been present at the Military Government scrutiny of the film, employed the narrow perspective of Hollywood as America's 'ambassador of goodwill' and proceeded to describe Wilder as 'crude, superficial and insensible to certain responsibilities.' It was Wilder's temerity in daring to criticize the United States ('a symbol of freedom') that enraged Herbert Luft, a refugee from Dachau. In the same magazine, Luft, associating Wilder's cinematic satire with Nazi philosophy, treated the director as an aberration, out of touch with 'the American way of thinking': 'Like many Germans, Wilder depicts only the weaknesses and shortcomings of the American people, ridicules their habits, but never senses the strikingly salubrious strength of this vibrantly young republic (sic).'[11] Predictably, *A Foreign Affair* is condemned by Luft as superficial, frivolous, and cynical.

Yet from the opening horizontal pan of a devastated Berlin, seen from the window of a plane by visiting congressmen (and one congresswoman), Wilder's film registers its marked superiority to those in the first batch of innocuous, undistinguished American films allowed into the Occupied Zone at the end of the war. As Stuart Schulberg admitted: 'This picture seemed to have everything: Wilder, Dietrich, and Berlin. One almost expected to see the old UFA trade-mark in the main title.'[12] Indeed, on one level, the film is an argument between the United States and an older Germany, between Hollywood and UFA.

The narrative builds to a conventional melodramatic climax, in which a hunted Nazi is killed, and an unconvincing happy ending which pairs Captain Pringle (John Lund) and the recently 'defrosted' Congresswoman Frost (Jean Arthur). Yet the fate of Erika von Schlütow (Marlene Dietrich) is consciously made ambiguous, in the context of wily European woman and naïve, impressionable American Military Police. While the use of authentic contemporary locations was becoming popular in Hollywood, the *film noir*, which created a sombre, even menacing, atmosphere, had been developed in the USA largely by German or Austrian emigrés, including Wilder himself. The complexity of the film evident in the style also extends to both theme and characterization. Wilder derives considerable amusement from demonstrating that the charge of 'moral malaria' among GIs is justifiable. However, on grounds of pragmatism he defends the Occupation forces, using Colonel Plummer as mouthpiece in his address to the delegation:

> There is still a lot of hunger – but there is a new will to live. We had to build schools and find teachers and then teach the teachers. We have helped them to start a free press and institute a parliamentary government. They've just had their first free elections in fourteen years . . . It was like handing the village drunk a glass of water. What I want to point out is that it's a tough, thankless, lonely job. We're trying to lick it as well as we can.

Above all, the polarities were established through the film's female stars, Jean Arthur and Marlene Dietrich. The characters they acted out resonated with significances derived from the cinematic personae of the actresses. Each had become a national representative. Jean Arthur's congresswoman (the leading female characters are both professionals) was a natural extension of her roles for Frank Capra in the thirties. The part was written for her, but Wilder and Brackett had to persuade her to come out of voluntary retirement. As in *Mister Deeds Goes to Town* (Columbia, 1936), the hard edge of her independence and determination is softened by her small-town, rural origins and consequently by a lack of sophistication. Miss Frost's celebration of Iowa in song set beside Frau von Schlütow's caustic cabaret lyrics provides a further example of the basic contrast. Under Wilder's direction, the absurd idealism of James Stewart's senator in *Mister Smith Goes to Washington* (Columbia, 1939) is replaced here by something closer to puritanism and impractical moral absolutism. These traits are eventually subdued as Miss Frost, in the more relaxed moral atmosphere of Berlin, is encouraged to acknowledge her own femininity. A similar process is at work in *Ninotchka* (Paramount, 1939), on which Wilder had been a scriptwriter and which was released in Berlin and other parts of Germany to enthusiastic audiences in 1948.

Marlene Dietrich, for her part, had come to personify for American audiences the archetypal European temptress, subtle, sensuous, and sophisticated. Her typical air of mystery is here placed at the service of the plot: Erika von Schlütow is a woman with a past. Shaped by the star image industry of classic Hollywood (in *A Foreign Affair* she refers respectfully to 'the chic American woman' of Hollywood publicity), Dietrich is a paradox. On the one hand she had given wartime shows for GIs, always wearing khaki, refusing to allow pin-ups in uniform and, like the soldiers, eating out of mess tins and washing her face in snow. For this contribution to the war effort, she was awarded the Medal of Freedom. On screen, however, she remained independent, proud, and defiant. In *A Foreign Affair*, for instance, she does not become the property of the male protagonist. Her role is that of a cabaret singer (as in *The Blue Angel*, 1930) at the Lorelei night-club, the name suggesting a snare and seduction. It was with the songs for *The Blue Angel* that Dietrich began her collaboration with Friedrich Hollander, a German composer born in London. The partnership included the memorable 'See What the Boys in

35

the Back Room Will Have' for *Destry Rides Again* (Universal, 1939) as well as the cabaret numbers and the overall music score for *A Foreign Affair*. Hollander accompanied Dietrich's recording of the songs and played the pianist in the movie.

Erika von Schlütow is, then, both performer, her glamour and sexuality a spectacle for the audience, on screen and off, and a cultural symbol. Her bitter songs 'Illusions' and, especially, 'Black Market' communicate the *Weltschmerz* of Weimar Germany.

Black Market

Black market
Sneak around the corner – Budapesterstrasse
Black market
Peek around the corner – *la police qui passe*
Come, I'll show you things you cannot get elsewhere.
Come, make with the offers and you'll get your share.

Black market
Eggs for statuettes, smiles for cigarettes,
Got some broken down ideals? Like wedding rings? –
Ssh! Tiptoe!
Trade your things.

I'll trade you for your candy
Some gorgeous merchandise.
My camera, it's a dandy
Six by nine, just your size.
You want my porcelain figure?
A watch, a submarine?
A Rembrandt, salami, black lingerie from Wien?
I sell my goods – behind the screen.
No ceiling, no feeling,
A very smooth routine
You buy these goods
And boy! These goods – are keen . . .

Black market
Laces for the missus, chewing gum for kisses
Black market
Cuckoo clocks and bangles, thousand little angles
And see my little music box today.
Only six cartons,

Want to hear it play?
Black market
Mink and microscope for liverwurst and soap.
Browse around, I've got so many toys
Don't be bashful, step up boys.

You like my first edition
It's yours – that's how I am –
A simple definition:
You take art, I take Spam.
To you for your K-ration
Compassion – and maybe
An inkling, a twinkling of real sympathy.
I'm selling out. Take all I've got.
Ambitions, convictions, the works, why not?
Enjoy these goods
For boy, these goods – are *hot*.

Words and Music by Frederick Hollander
© 1948 Famous Music Corporation
Reproduced by permission of
Chappell Music Ltd., London
and Famous Music Corporation, New York

A Foreign Affair stands out as one of Wilder's most accomplished films, briskly paced and achieving a range of moods by means of *mise-en-scene* and skilful black and white photography. Its dialogue is brash and witty, recalling the screwball comedies of the late thirties such as *Ball of Fire* (RKO, 1941), a screenplay by Wilder and Brackett. The two men – Brackett, a Harvard Law School graduate, drama critic and novelist, urbane and respectable, and Wilder, the one-time tea-dance gigolo, cynical and acerbic – complemented each other perfectly. Their successful partnership as scenario writers and as a producer-director team earned them the title 'Hollywood's Happiest Couple'.

Official disapproval notwithstanding, *A Foreign Affair* was a commercial triumph in the USA. *Time* magazine may have found it 'too inhumane' while the *Saturday Review* expressed the standard negative attitude: 'The trials and tribulations of Berlin are not the stuff of which cheap comedy is made and rubble makes lousy custard pies.'[13] However, Bosley Crowther in the *New York Times* praised the direction, script, and acting, and the *Motion Picture Herald* recommended it to exhibitors as 'swell entertainment' with 'nary a dull moment' (19 June 1948). An unprepared audience at a Los Angeles preview rated it excellent and subsequent audiences came to the same conclusion. At the Paramount Theater, New York, for example, *A Foreign Affair* broke all records for the Fourth of July weekend.

On its release the movie proved to be entertaining, the quality cogently advocated by its director in 1945. On his way to Berlin in that year, Wilder was engaged to supervise the cutting of Hanus Burger's concentration camp documentary, *Todesmühlen* (Death Mills), an activity which has generated some controversy.[14] Michael Hoenisch has persuasively related Wilder's ruthless editing to the privileging of fiction films in 'Propaganda through Entertainment'.[15]

Whatever Wilder's views on re-education through film were in 1945, the kind of film proposed was not made. *A Foreign Affair* (1948), on the other hand, sees re-education as ill-conceived. One of the fascinations of the film is the mixture of materials and perspectives from those years. Wilder retains certain references from his memorandum: the realistic view of the GI expounded by Captain Pringle and the anecdote about the woman yearning for gas with which to commit suicide, used by Colonel Plummer in his address to the delegation. However, the Cold War has intensified since 1945, so Plummer also refers to the beginnings of democracy in Germany. The foundation of a Federal Republic and re-armament are just around the corner.

It is in the composite figure of Marlene Dietrich/Erika von Schlütow, however, that the 1945 and 1948 materials are commingled most effectively. Erika in microcosm represents recent German history. As the mistress of a leading Nazi official she is admitted to Hitler's company; in wartime she suffers like her compatriots:

> Bombed out a dozen times, everything caved in and pulled out from under me, my country, my possessions, my beliefs. Yet somehow I kept going. Months and months in air-raid shelters, crammed in with five thousand other people. I kept going . . . It was a living hell.

Her determination and sexy allure have ensured her survival during the Occupation. This history is recapitulated in the rousing song (delivered in German – and French and Russian – as well as English), 'The Ruins of Berlin', which refers to 'the phantoms of the past', 'all your sorrows' (post-war privations), and 'a sweet tomorrow'. Dietrich wore her own clothes to authenticate the drab period of the film, but with Hollander's assistance she prophesies the national resurgence and economic boom of the fifties: 'A brand new spring is to begin / Out of the ruins of Berlin.'

The Wilder Memorandum

HEADQUARTERS   BW/aoc
UNITED STATES FORCES, EUROPEAN THEATER
Information Control Division
APO 757, U.S. ARMY

SUBJECT: Propaganda through Entertainment. 16 August 1945
TO: Mr Davidson Taylor

1. So now we are slowly opening up the movie houses in Germany. We are showing them our documentaries, some facts we want them to know and to remember well. We are showing them newsreels which carry along with the news a lesson, a reminder, and a warning. A good job has been done, no doubt. Germans on the whole are receptive and the overall reaction is favorable. Attendance ranges from capacity to satisfactory. And yet we all realize that once this novelty has worn off (in Berlin it has worn off already) we shall find it increasingly difficult to deliver our lessons straight. Will the Germans come in week after week to play the guilty pupil? Sure enough we will be showing them our feature films, pure entertainment along with the documentaries. They will come in alright. Only we may find them dozing apathetically through these documentaries and educational newsreels – to be bright and ready for Rita Hayworth in COVER GIRL. COVER GIRL is a fine film, mind you. It has a love story, it has music and it is in technicolor. However, it does not particularly help us in our program of re-educating the German people. Now *if* there was an entertainment film with Rita Hayworth or Ingrid Bergman or Gary Cooper, in Technicolor if you wish, and with a love story – only with a very special love story, cleverly devised to help us sell a few ideological items – such a film would provide us with a superior piece of propaganda: they would stand in long lines to buy and once they bought it, it would stick. Unfortunately, no such film exists yet. It must be made. I want to make it.

2. In 1940 you remember – during the London blitz – people in the States had to be told that there was a real war on, that England was hanging in the ropes and that she was desperately in need of our help. Newsreels did their share and we were quite impressed by such English documentaries as TARGET FOR TONIGHT. But I think it took a Hollywood film – an 'entertainment film'

based on a fictitious story – to really tell us what was going on. And that what was happening to the Minniver [*sic*] family in England could easily happen to the Jones family in Iowa. As a matter of fact, President Roosevelt having seen the first print of MRS. MINIVER urged Metro to put the film on the market as quickly as possible. They rushed it out. It did a job no documentary, no 50 newsreels could have done.

3. Films like MRS. MINIVER or the one I am suggesting can only be made by a professional motion picture company. They must be made on the highest possible level as far as technique, writing, casting, etc., are concerned. Such a film would cost around 1½ million dollars. We have approached the group of touring motion picture executives during their stay in Bad Homburg with this idea, and they showed interest. There were further discussions on this subject with the Hollywood people in Paris. Paramount's Mr. Balaban and Mr. Holman felt that Paramount should be the one to do the film since I am on a long term contract to them and only 'on a temporary loan to the U.S. Government'. They would consider it unfair if I went out and made the film for another commercial company. I myself am all for it – I have worked at Paramount for nine straight years and have written and directed a string of pictures. I know the staff and the crews and I don't think that any other Hollywood company could possibly give me more freedom of action. They will be willing to give me top stars, the best staff and a budget of 1½ million to do the film.

4. As you know, it is a very simple story of an American G.I. stationed here with the occupational troops and a German Fraulein, or I should say, a German Frau, because her husband, an Oberleutnant in the Luftwaffe, has been killed in action over Tunisia. I have met such a Frau in Berlin – she was working in a bucket brigade cleaning up the rubble on Kurfurstendamm. I had thrown away a cigarette and she had picked up the butt. We started a conversation. Here it is: 'I am so glad you Americans have finally come because . . .' 'Because what?' 'Because now you will help us repair the gas.' 'Sure we will.' 'That's all we are waiting for, my mother and I . . .' 'I suppose it will be nice to get a warm meal again.' 'It is not to cook . . .' There was a long pause. I kind of felt what she meant, and I wished she would not say it. She did. 'We will turn it on, but we won't light it. Don't you see! It is just to

breathe it in, deep.' 'Why do you say that?' 'Why? Because we Germans have nothing to live for any more.' 'If you call living for Hitler a life, I guess you are right.' I held out a brand new Lucky Strike to her. She did not take it. She just picked up the bucket and went back to the rubble.

Right here in this piece of dialogue is the theme of the picture, and here is the simple ending I want to arrive at: when the gas finally *is* turned on our German Frau strikes a match to cook her dinner, a few measly potatoes I grant you – but now that a few facts have dawned on her she has 'something new to live for'. This is what the film should state (in Eisenhower's words): 'That we are not here to degrade the German people but to make it impossible to wage war' – and in the end 'let us give them a little hope to redeem themselves in the eyes of the world'.

As for the G.I., I shall not make him a flag waving hero or a theorizing apostle of democracy. As a matter of fact, in the beginning of the picture I want him not to be too sure of what the hell this was all about. I want to touch on fraternization, on homesickness, on black market. Furthermore, (although, it is a 'love story') boy does *not* get girl. He goes back home with his division while the girl he leaves behind 'sees the light'. There shall be no pompous messages. Let me quote you another piece of dialogue I ran into in Berlin. I had a German driver and this is the kind of dialogue that would develop between us: 'About this British election – now that this Atlee has defeated Churchill, what is Churchill going to do?' 'I guess he will stay in politics. Or he will write a book, or paint.' 'Maybe he is going to make a Putsch, nicht wahr?' 'I don't think so.' 'You mean he is not even going to shoot Atlee?' 'No, he is not.' 'Are you sure?' 'Look man, Wilkie did not make a Putsch against Roosevelt and Dewey did not shoot Truman.' 'That's funny.' 'It's hilarious, it's democratic!' I want to put such stuff into the film because I think it has just the right texture to say things without preaching.

5. I have spent two weeks in Berlin (working on a report about future German film production). I found the town mad, depraved, starving, fascinating as a background for a movie. My notebooks are filled with hot research stuff. I have photographed every corner I need for atmosphere. I have talked to General Gavin, the Commanding General of the 82nd Airborne Division, now the

main occupying U.S. troops in Berlin; he assured me of every cooperation. I have lived with some of his G.I.'s and put down their lingo. I have talked to Russian WACs and British M.P.'s. I have fraternized with Germans, from bombed out university professors to three cigarette-chippies at the Femina. I have almost sold my wristwatch at the black market under the Reichstag. I have secured the copyrights to the famous song *'Berlin kommt wieder'*. I think I am quite ready now to sit down with my collaborator and start writing the script.

6. The film should be made in just *one* version, the Americans speaking English and broken German, the Germans speaking German and broken English, the Russians speaking Russian, etc. If necessary, we can put in occasional titles, but I shall try making it all as natural as possible. Once the script is finished it shall be submitted to the War Department in Washington. I also want to send a copy to this Division for its approval. The film shall be shot in Hollywood, that is the interiors which will comprise about 85% of the film. The exteriors will be shot in Berlin, they will be silent and only a skeleton crew of some 8 men and the 2 stars will be needed here. I figure we will have to spend some 3 weeks in Berlin to get these shots. If transportation in Europe cannot be obtained through the Army, I could also do the exteriors in Hollywood by using process shots.

7. Together with this memorandum, I am handing in a report on future German picture production. In my opinion, no production of German pictures is possible in the near future. It will take some time to vet prospective producers, to assemble stars, writers, directors and crews. As for the equipment, most of it has been stolen or destroyed. I should think that there will be no new German films made for the next eight or ten months. As we are not here to produce films ourselves, but only to *control* the ones the Germans will be producing, I am suggesting in my report that we shall find a man who will be sitting in Berlin, together with the British and Russians, and whose job it will be to read all proposed scripts, to check on policy and to watch out that no Fascist thought or Nazi propaganda gets on their celluloid. I don't think that the Division will need me for this kind of passive job. As for the distribution end, we have now with us Mr. Schwartz and Mr. Joseph, two extremely able men who can handle that sort of stuff

very much better than I (having never very much bothered about anything but the actual making of films). I frankly feel that my further stay in Bad Homburg would be stealing money from the Government.

8. If I should be given a quickly go ahead signal on my film project, I think I could place the finished product sometime early next year into General McClure's hands to show it to the German people. I am conceited enough to say that you will find this 'entertainment' film the best propaganda yet.

BILLY WILDER

Chapter four

Art and Architecture: From Wasteland to Late Modernism

Painting

Of all the arts, painting appeared most unrelated to anything happening in America in 1945–6. There was, though, one special case, for, in the late forties, the painter Max Beckmann was to be filled with hope and vigour by the optimism and vitality of the United States. The awe-inspiring imagery of the West and the throbbing energy of New York City, where he liked to explore Chinatown and the Bowery, inspired in his work bold forms and strong colours. Two paintings in particular demonstrate the perspective of the immigrant: *Landscape in Boulder* (1949), with its austere, inaccessible black rocks, and *San Francisco* (1950), a vividly coloured panorama in which the city visibly vibrates. Having taken up a chair at Washington University Art School in 1947, Beckmann died in New York in 1950 on the way to the Metropolitan Museum to see his *Self Portrait in Blue Jacket*.

Brainwashed by Nazi views of 'degenerate' art, the German public was slow to respond to modern painting and they were given little encouragement by the universities, where a conservative opposition was growing. In the art world itself there was still much talk of 'the people' and 'the nation', but a craving for information about culture and art abroad was soon evident. Free exhibitions were set up in makeshift galleries, some supplied by artists who travelled around the country with water colours, oils, and even small sculptures in their knapsacks. International developments when known were intensively studied and discussed, particularly in places where the art journals of an America House or comparable institution were available: Allied officers of culture were firm in their support for 'education in modern art'.

The first post-war private gallery in Germany was opened in Berlin in August 1945 and the opening address, 'On the Freedom of Art', was given by the historian Edwin Redslob, later Rector of the Free University of Berlin. More important were the actions of Hilla von Rebay which exemplified a widespread definition of democracy as both cultural influence and practical generosity. Von Rebay, a German-American, had studied and fostered abstract art in Germany in the twenties and later became the first director of the Guggenheim in New York. After the war, she chose fifty works of modern art from the Guggenheim collection for a travelling exhibition that went to Stuttgart, Munich, Hamburg, Braunschweig and Düsseldorf, as well as a number of European capitals. However, having seen the conditions in post-war Munich, she also sent CARE packages to the painters there.

Some museums displayed examples of expressionism again and recalled other modern German traditions (as in the 'Masters of the Bauhaus' exhibition, Berlin, 1947), but such issues as Germany's artistic history or possible reactions to the Zero Hour situation received relatively little attention. The problem, for instance, of capturing in art the kind of mass destruction represented by concentration camps and the atomic bomb was a real one and similar historical questions would still preoccupy German artists in the seventies. The landscapes of craters and rubble were themselves like a giant surrealistic painting. Werner Heldt capitalized artistically on that perception. He painted a stark, post-apocalyptic Berlin, presenting it as a sombre city, scarred by war and death, deserted, empty of life; at the same time his *Berlin-by-the-sea* pictures of ruins and dunes could give the effect of a tidal wave. The most typical and most significant pictures painted in the immediate post-war period were, in the opinion of the critic Wieland Schmied, 'those created by loners in situations of great isolation'.[1] This surely has to include the Berlin sequences of Heldt, an ex-prisoner of war, an outsider, and an alcoholic. The deeply pessimistic work of Karl Hofer which bears such titles as *Totentanz* (Dance of Death) and *Atomserenade* portrayed individuals as doomed and spiritually lost even if, as in *Die Blinden*, four people are able to cling to each other as they grope through a forest of dead trees. For the artists of the time the survivors of the war were like victims of a shipwreck drifting through an amorphous world that was both dream and reality.

In contrast to the narrow rigidity of Nazi art, a plurality of styles flourished and diversification was still evident by 1949–50. In 1949 the abstract painters Willi Baumeister, Fritz Winter, and Ernest Nay were shown along with Max Beckmann, Max Bechstein, and Otto Dix at Cologne's 'Contemporary German Sculpture and Painting' exhibition. The work of Baumeister and Winter had been considered outmoded just after the war when it was fashionable to reject expressionism as belonging to Germany's violent and sordid past.

Much more popular at the time was the quasi-modernist style of 'magic realism' which mystified political questions and rendered Fascism, the Second World War, and national defeat as incomprehensible shocks or apocalyptic disasters created by Nature. Like certain European and American plays of the period, this was an existential art focused on a personal struggle with outside forces, especially fate. The fearful and tense humanism that accompanied the realistic style was an authentic response to the new age of nuclear weapons, but realism, and with it references to a German tradition of which 'magic realism' and 'new objectivity' were part, faded in the fifties as the Cold War dictated aesthetic forms. Regarded as evidence of cultural (and political) immaturity it was consigned to the Eastern Bloc. West Germany, on the other hand, in its enthusiasm for the rich colours and exciting shapes of abstract art, was not only proclaiming its sophistication, but was saying goodbye to the dreariness of Zero Hour. It was also making clear its identity, allegiances, and desires.[2]

> Abstraction seemed to be the logical and definitive
> consequence of the developments in art history since
> Cezanne . . . German artists in particular regarded the
> language of abstraction as a moral force which was
> internationally binding as well as promoting international
> friendship. Germany above all yearned for internationality, it
> yearned to be accepted once again into the fold of nations
> and to be recognised as an equal partner.[3]

The years 1947 and 1948 were important for abstraction in art as it moved towards the position of hegemony it achieved in the fifties. A study by Ottamar Domnick in 1947, *Creative Forces in Abstract Painting*, championed Baumeister, whose own text *The Unknown in Art* in the same year sought to make abstraction (as vision and mysticism) palatable to the Church. Also, in contrast to the Nazi theory of so-called 'Art for the People', Baumeister described the artist as a single separate member of an elite, speaking to other, equally free creative individuals. Later, in the following decade, the individualism of American artists would be co-opted in order to combat the authoritarianism of Soviet collectivism.

Initially the literary term *Kahlschlag*, implying an austere, stripped-down effect had seemed an appropriate term for the realism of post-war art, but in 1948 Leopold Zahn in the magazine *Das Kunstwerk* (Motto: Dedicated to Abstract Painting) announced: 'The Age of Mimesis is over: the taste for abstract art prevails all over the world.' Except perhaps in the USSR which incurred Zahn's hostility for its opposition to abstraction, the year 1948 also marked the virtual end of open debate about aesthetics and politics in the United States. Stephen Spender published his influential article, 'We can win the battle for the mind of Europe' in the *New York Times Magazine* of 25 April 1948 (VI, p. 15), and the exhibition 'Non-Representational Painting in America' toured several German cities, proclaiming American power and freedom. It also offered German artists their chance of cultural emulation, the opportunity to become integrated into the Western art scene, despite the absence in Germany of a real art capital like Paris or New York.

Architecture

The term 'the rubble years' is a reminder of the persistence after the war of bombed out cityscapes with some ruins, usually churches, preserved as memorials, and also of the pressing needs for family housing and business premises. The key words were improvisation and immediacy. Improvised stalls that served as shops were known as Baracks (a combination of Baroque and barracks). An element of the *ad hoc* was to remain even after 1948 when, with a market in building materials once more in operation, free-for-all competition started to transform the appearance of cities by means of office blocks, stores, cinemas, hotels, and those symbols of security and success, insurance offices.

At first, however, the work of reconstruction was rushed: time was too valuable to be spent on the luxury of research. Occasionally rebuilding was speeded up to make a statement. The restoration of St Paul's Church, Frankfurt, where Parliament's bill of rights was drawn up in 1848, was given priority as a democratic gesture. The centenary celebration attended by representatives of the US Military Government was held at the church, still draped in scaffolding, and the event was the front-page headline and story in the *Frankfurter Rundschau* of 20 May 1948. Generally the air of crisis and haste was responsible for conventional functional buildings. Military defeat had withered national self-confidence: the mental vacuum and despair noted by visitors could encourage little by way of innovation. The style of reconstruction, therefore, was dictated in the first instance by caution. Mediocrity in architecture was demonstrably not confined to Germany in this period; nevertheless Hubert Hoffmann could with justification complain in 1956: 'In town and country alike the shapeless, the very dull predominate by far.'[4] It was not that such new buildings provoked judgements in terms of beauty or ugliness; rather, they stood within a narrow spectrum of anonymity.

There were essentially two approaches to the reconstruction of Germany. The first, functional modernism, aligned itself with the ideas of those German exiles associated with the international style. Their main contemporary disciple was Hans Scharoun, who directed the post-war planning of West Berlin. During a series of lectures in Germany sponsored by the Military Government and delivered by Walter Gropius, Scharoun was singled out for praise as an architect and planner. Gropius also reinstated a central Bauhaus idea of a socially conscious architecture symbolizing freedom and individuality. The year was 1947, the year of the Marshall Plan and the Truman Doctrine.

In the same year, though, Heinrich Tessenow articulated a very different architectural doctrine, moving into the foreground the need to preserve the past and restore old city centres. Naturally the immediate past was regarded with nervous suspicion or total aversion: the regional, provincial style of building had, along with neo-classicism, been perverted to create the architecture of the Third Reich. Tessenow and others were more concerned with authentic city 'planning', with the proportions and configurations characteristic of ancient towns, and most of all, with scrapping any proposed solutions arrived at in the interests of road traffic. The significance for Germans of the forest as a spiritual symbol makes it easier for us to understand their love of trees and parks. A more practical application of an otherwise sentimental attachment has been in land use and the defence of greenbelts, often through the placing of restrictions on private exploitation and development.

In cities and towns, however, the record is patchy. Historical restoration has taken place with bombed areas rebuilt according to surviving street plans. In Frankfurt the *Römer* (the old quarter) and the *Goethehaus* were swiftly reconstructed, the latter to the original specifications, 'even down to the warped floorboards and the crooked frames' as a character in David Lodge's *Out of the Shelter* reports. Elsewhere, as in the United States, urban planning has been fainthearted in its resistance to the automobile and subservient in its relationship with commerce. Politicians and local officials displayed little vision, while in some instances ideologists of the Third Reich continued to sit on the committees of recon-struction authorities.

American influence upon German architecture begins in the early years of the century with the work of Frank Lloyd Wright and continues after the Second World War when renewed contacts were made with German architects who had emigrated to the United States as a refuge from the Third Reich: Wagner, Hil-berseimer, Mendelsohn, Wachsmann, and Neutra, but above all Gropius and Mies van der Rohe. Gropius, who represented the beginning and culmination of the Bauhaus, designed a house in Hanover in 1953, Mies submitted a design to the competition for Mannheim's *Nationaltheater*, and both were involved in appro-priate Berlin activities, but their *direct* intervention in German architecture after the war was strictly limited. The same could not be said for their influence.

Although Mies had no real students in post-war Germany he had many admirers, who produced too many feeble stucco imit-ations of his style. Gradually more and more American firms undertook commissions and in this way German architects, engineers and planners came under the modernist spell that combined glass, steel, and pre-stressed concrete. As in America, so in Germany, the glass box and the curtain wall became standard elements in the design of new office buildings. (The curtain wall was no immigrant as the Bauhaus workshop at Dessau, 1925–6, testifies.) Lewis Mumford described Miesian buildings as elegant monuments of nothingness and many examples were open to the charges of expensive, nondescript similarity and insufficient concern for site, climate, and the needs of inhabitants. Given the pressure for post-war reconstruction, the simple modular form, and the rigidity and absolutism of Miesian rules, the adoption of modernism was predictable. The results, not least in Germany, were also predictable and often disastrous.

National predilections and cultural preferences did not disappear. Some tall skyscrapers arose in German cities (the tallest was the BASF skyscraper in Ludwigshafen) but the separate ownership of buildings limited such tendencies. Medium-sized, relatively low urban structures were the traditional norm in Germany and Central Europe, so in many instances new commercial buildings were modest, displayed a sense of urban scale, and even blended with older buildings. Some of the best new German architecture (in Berlin, Hamburg, and Düsseldorf) was remarkably small by American standards.

> Only now, and very slowly, do office blocks and
> administrative buildings begin to dominate the skyline of our
> towns, as they do in the United States, where they have long
> been . . . a symbol of economic power . . . Office blocks
> have so far had to conform with the frontages and heights of
> the rest of the street.(1956)[5]

While Americans were better at constructing airports and weekend country hotels, Germans could point with pride to theatres and leisure centres. Mies van der Rohe attempted to express a central difference: 'We [Americans] are free, we can do what we like. The Germans have a historical tradition – it could give them strength, but at the same time it is a limitation.'[6]

If there was an identifiable dichotomy then it was between the crafted building (German) and the industrialized building (American). At the end of the war expert workmanship was still cheap in Germany, so that a door or window with special proportions would cost no more than a standard one. The details of curtain walls could be perfected. However, the erection of apartment houses necessitated the use of American mass production methods and, as the case for making economies became more urgent (with labour costs increasing), so pre-planning and pre-engineering in the American style were adopted more readily.

One of the most important of pre-planning organizations with its motto of 'Programming is Function' was the American architectural firm of Skidmore, Owings, and Merrill. Before 1950 its approach to design owed more to Gropius than Mies, but in any case it embraced the impersonality of the international style which the German exiles had helped to create. The sheer size of the firm, over 1,000 staff in the mid-fifties, was a portent for the future of architectural practice. Thus, the committee style planning of Berlin's *Hansaviertel* by Interbau (over a dozen German architects and several from abroad) in 1956–8 should be regarded in the context of an increase in size and rationalized organization.

It was in the construction of buildings with a specific Occupation purpose – consulates, information centres, apartments for government employees – that Skidmore, Owings, and Merrill specialized. Its most notable monuments, however, were completed after the formation of the Federal Republic. Prominent among these were flats in Bremen for workers at the American Consulate (in keeping with the expansion in the early fifties of the United States presence in Germany outside the old American zone); the admired Miesian consulate in Frankfurt, along with living quarters, a school, and a kindergarten; and the *Amerika-Institut* of Frankfurt's Goethe-University with its special room put at the disposal of exchange professors from the University of Chicago.

In its consulate work Skidmore, Owings, and Merrill employed the Frankfurt architect Otto Appel, a collaboration which gave Germans the chance to absorb the latest developments. Once the practice was adopted, however the Germans needed no instruction in order to plump for Miesian solutions as avidly as the Americans: witness the Stuttgart Parliament, the Cologne Kaufhof store, or the addition to the Mannesmann building in Düsseldorf. Nevertheless, there was an architectural sense of mission present in the early fifties, at least in the State Department. Its Office of Foreign Buildings Operations started a construction programme in 1952 aimed at housing government workers as well as advertising current American trends in architecture.

Unfortunately American trends in town planning also established themselves. The rebuilding of German cities offered opportunities, too often refused, to rescue city space from the incursions of cars and roads. Unsightly car parks, easily made from vacant land cleared of wartime rubble, began to proliferate. Some cities did opt for building imaginative walkways, arcades, and bridges; but with pedestrian precincts opposed by commercial interests, attempts to create and design enclosed places secure from traffic were relatively few. The unwillingness to proceed patiently through the business of acquiring private property in order to widen streets or remove bottlenecks was symptomatic of utilitarian post-war attitudes. Architects slipped back into the role of consumers applying concepts of design rather than creating them.

Hans Scharoun's new street plan for Berlin preserved little of the historical city, just the centre and, appropriately, the museum area. The emphasis was to be on parallel and perpendicular highways serving the residential and business districts and aiming to check the American-style drift to the suburbs. In two particular instances opportunities were lost. At Ernst Reuter Platz, a large traffic circle lined with business offices, the central green space was imprisoned by cars. These could have been routed underground or a solution using terraces and walkways could have been sought. The area 'round and about the Zoo', also in Berlin, and a conglomeration of traffic and diverse public and private facilities was the subject of a competition in 1948. Several of the schemes submitted, including pedestrianization, flyover roads and single-storey shops would have ameliorated the chaotic traffic conditions. None was adopted. Similarly, innovative plans for Magdeburg (1945), Emden (1947), and Nuremberg (1947) remained on paper.

The motives for modernized 'city organisms' were not simply commercial but social and ideological as well. Scharoun's kind of urban architecture was perceived as a symbol of freedom and individualism, a mirror of an optimistic, progressive, democratic society opened up to sunlight and fresh air and with its sights clearly directed towards the future. A belief in technology would help to confirm the presence of a progressive spirit, one turned away from provincialism, folkishness, the past, and National Socialism. The eager acceptance of international modernism in physical form was part of the project to find a cultural and civilized identity and persuade other nations still conscious of Germany's Nazi past to discard their image of her as pariah of the modern world.

Chapter five

Fiction and Drama: That's Entertainment!

The American novel

At the end of the war Germans were obliged to add a paucity (and rationing) of reading material to their other deprivations. In Heidelberg books could be bought only on the black market, while in Bremen queues at bookshops and newspaper stands were longer than breadlines. Some of the old publishers such as Insel, Reclam, Suhrkamp-Fischer, and Rowohlt started operating again, but in October 1945 licensed book dealers outnumbered publishers by a ratio of over a hundred to one. Brochures and pamphlets were the standard model for the printed word. The book trade itself was severely hampered by the loss of pre-war stock, an unstable currency, restrictions on materials, particularly paper, and elementary postal difficulties. The reading of books has been a more firmly established and honoured tradition in Germany than in the United States. Now everything in print – if not sold before publication – was enthusiastically seized from popular novels such as *Forever Amber* and *A Tree Grows in Brooklyn* to the first issue (20,000 copies) of *Die Amerikanische Rundschau* with its serious articles on history, politics, and philosophy.

American literature in the form of novels by Dreiser, Sinclair, Anderson, Hemingway, and Wolfe had been well received in Germany before the war. Critics of the United States welcomed the work of Sinclair Lewis as confirmation that across the Atlantic was a nation of Babbitts; supporters held to a vision of a literature commensurate with the resources and territorial size of the USA. By 1937 an article in the *American–German Review* could bear the title, 'American literature conquers Germany'. Despite the war,

American titles continued to find their way to Europe through Pocket Books Inc., overseas editions, and, of course, Armed Forces editions.

In the decade following 1945 over 1,400 works of American prose fiction were published in German editions. The writings of Poe, Hawthorne, and, especially, Melville continued to attract German readers; literary history of the Romántic period in the USA (1815–65) was provided by Van Wyck Brooks's Pulitzer Prize winning book *The Flowering of New England* (1936). Among other early translations published in the American zone were Morison and Commager's *The Growth of the American Republic* (1930), Sandburg's history of Lincoln during the Civil War years (*Storm Over the Land*, 1942), and Margaret Mead's anthropological analysis of America, *Keep Your Powder Dry* (1942). The publication in 1946 of three books on Walt Whitman and a reprinting of Benjamin Franklin's autobiography in the same year were further evidence of a desire to investigate American culture. Whitman's faith in democracy and Franklin's advocacy of the Protestant work ethic were by no means out of place in a Germany anxious to rebuild for the future.

Young German readers and writers were at the very least ambivalent towards their own history and cultural traditions. In any case the older generation of wartime writers had either emigrated or had been persuaded by events to write within narrow thematic confines: accounts of Nazi persecution, for instance. From 1945 and Zero Hour onwards the young responded positively to the modernity and freshness of American narrative: like Hemingway (a favourite in Germany) they belonged to a 'lost generation' disillusioned by a cataclysmic war and wavering between nihilism and humanism. The time was ripe for a literary invasion.

American novels, with their energy, their colourful colloquial language, and their naturalistic detail, stripping modern life of illusion, had a special appeal in addition to the obvious one of political expediency. These literary qualities did not preclude humour and optimism. Even those nationalistic critics who regarded much American writing as crude or superficial could not resist the powerful prose style everywhere evident. Supplies of books gradually improved and by 1950 American Pocket Books, displayed throughout West Germany, helped to satisfy the demand for cheap editions of contemporary American literature. Equally important as an influence on behalf of American writing and modern literature generally was the Hamburg publisher Ernst Rowohlt, who decided to abandon the conventional book form and to use newspaper printed on rotary machines. His 32-page booklets, printed in columns and selling at 50 pfennigs each, were published in editions of 100,000 and were the beginnings of the *rororo* paperback enterprise. Among American authors featured were Hergesheimer, Lewis (*Dodsworth*), Faulkner (*Light in August*), and Hemingway, whose *For Whom the Bell Tolls* was among the first to be published.

The printed word could provide that knowledge of the outside world which had been withheld from Germans for a decade. It was for this reason that the anthropological and geographical information in the *National Geographic Magazine* was so sought after by English-speaking Germans. Moreover, Dos Passos and Steinbeck approached the popularity of Hemingway not solely for their concern with what was perceived as the universal 'human condition' but also because of the light they cast upon aspects of American social and regional life.

The Austrian periodical *Das Silberboot* rated Thomas Wolfe equal in significance with Fitzgerald and Hemingway; and in 1947 Rowohlt was making plans to reissue *Look Homeward, Angel*, originally published in a German version in 1933. The appeal of this romantic work lay in its hopefulness and its liberal belief in freedom, democracy, and individualism. Similarly, *You Can't Go Home Again* which, translated into German, appeared in Switzerland during the early forties, embraces at its conclusion an inspiring vision of true democracy. Perhaps you can't 'go home' again in the accepted sense of the phrase, but home really lies in the future. Wolfe's confident optimism placed him in the tradition of Thoreau and Whitman, so his novels came to be regarded as incorporating the spirit of an authentic America, not just a world of skyscrapers and neon but a varied, vital, and progressive country. Otto Knapp, writing for *Frankfurter Hefte* in August 1947, made that very point in an article '*Idealistisches Amerika*' which traced the liberal heritage back to New England Puritanism and Harvard University.

A more puzzling case than Wolfe's is that of Jack London, a considerable number of whose books were translated into

German. Despite his sympathy for the Jews, London's attraction to the blonde superman of Nietzsche, his celebration of primitive strength, his belief in Aryan unity, and his archetypal Wagnerian women (one is named Saxon) hardly equipped him to be an instrument of democratic re-education. Even his most left-wing book, *The Iron Heel* (translated 1948), predicts the failure of socialism and the inexorable rise of Fascism. By 1948, however, denazification was in decline and London's books had after all been burned and banned in Hitler's Germany.

Realism was a *sine qua non*, especially the depiction, against the background of the global spiritual crisis, of what one German critic listed as 'chaos, fear, hate, decay, resistance and the evil and noble forces in man'. The Germans had a word for it: *Wirklichkeitsnähe*, 'an unfalsified atmosphere of a critical, responsible and unprovincial bent'.[1] In American literature that truthfulness was seen to co-exist with idealism, a humanitarian unsentimental idealism of the kind many discovered in Hemingway's *For Whom the Bell Tolls* (translated 1948 and 1949).

After 1945 nearly all the works of Hemingway, who was easy to read in German, were translated. His recognition of basic truths and the absence of embellishments in his style and of illusions in his male protagonists struck a chord in the stoic consciousness of a ravaged Germany. If this was Zero Hour, Hemingway described life at zero or *Nullpunktexistenz*. A contributor to *Der Ruf*, Gustav Rene Hocke, advocated in his article '*Deutsche Kalligraphie*' the style of *Kahlschlag* (literally deforestation) – that is, a simple realism reflecting the deprivations of post-war life. *Kahlschlagliteratur* was encouraged, though not to the exclusion of other styles, by 'Group 47', a band of nonconformist writers which assumed the mantle of *Der Ruf*. The first piece of literature to be read and discussed by the group was a contribution from the prose writer Wolfdietrich Schnurre, an exponent of precision and succinctness; the tale in question, 'The Funeral' (1946) shows a distinct affinity with the style of Hemingway. One of the participants in the discussion suggested afterwards that the spirits of Gertrude Stein and Hemingway had been present in the room, inspiring them to stick to austere, declarative language, clear, direct, and anti-bourgeois. Schnurre's sardonic realism restricted the manifesting of emotions, but the short story was also a suitable vehicle for registering directly those feelings experienced by so many at the end of the war: fear, loneliness, alienation.

The American short story, which characteristically offered its readers psychological depth and unity of tone and atmosphere, was a powerful influence upon German writers. Hemingway's stories, among them 'The Killers' and 'The Undefeated', were published as early as 1945 in the collection which took another tale for its title: 'The Snows of Kilimanjaro'. This volume included 'Big Two-Hearted River' which Malcolm Cowley, in an essay translated into German two years later, was to interpret as the product of a traumatized nocturnal spirit resembling Poe or Hawthorne.[2] Interest in Hemingway both as man and writer was reflected in the rapid re-publication of his novels: *A Farewell to Arms* in 1946, *The Sun Also Rises* (1947), and in 1948 *For Whom the Bell Tolls*, which in its presentation of fortitude and its anti-Fascism appeared to make a fictional contribution to the process of political re-education. Critics in the East, however, pointed out that Robert Jordan never fully embraces the cause of Communism. His condition is, in Wolfgang Joho's phrase, 'the isolation of weary non-commitment'. In the Western zones, on the other hand, Hemingway evoked a strong response to his descriptions of the terrors of existence and his explorations of the individual soul caught up in those terrors. With fear and *angst* at the centre of his work he seemed to articulate objectively the feelings and fate of an entire generation. However, while he clarified the German (and European) situation he also suggested that by the affirmation and practice of courage, sacrifice, and pride there was a future to be struggled for and won.

Other American books took the recent past for their theme. The success of fiction such as Norman Mailer's *The Naked and the Dead* and James Jones's *From Here to Eternity* demonstrated the presence in the German psyche of a fascination with, as well as an aversion to, the passage of war. The attraction of Mailer's epic was comprehensible, at least on one level. This was a Second World War novel which confirmed what most of its audience must already have known, often through experience: war is hell, violence in wartime is ubiquitous, and the army is a hateful and dehumanizing institution. The contemporary significance of the novel was underlined by Mailer's imaginative investigation of the Fascist mentality and the dramatization of Fascism as a system of social control.

General Cummings, Mailer's single-minded reactionary, obsessed with power, believes that history is in 'the grip of the right' – the novel provides no refutation of this idea – and echoes Hitler in announcing that 'the only morality of the future is power morality'.

If Mailer is interpreted as the ringer of alarm bells, warning of the dangers of post-war Fascism, the next question is: where does the possibility of heroic and effective resistance lie? The answer is extremely melancholy. Mailer inherits the determinism of the modern naturalist novel: since the stratification of the army is a paradigm of the contemporary world, it seems unlikely that the attempt of the Fascist, General Cummings, to enter the State Department by means of his wife's connections can be thwarted. The totalitarian alliance between the rational abstract Cummings and the irrational murderous Sergeant Croft, which destroys the liberal Lieutenant Hearn, is meant to refer symbolically to American politics and society. Thus, left-wing politics has no future in the United States or, for that matter, elsewhere in the West. Art, religion, comradeship, working-class solidarity – all are found to be impotent. Only the negative emotions of hatred, disgust, and prejudice are vivid and energetic. Mailer offers only a bleak environment (both politically and psychologically) and a future (like that in Orwell's contemporaneous novel *1984*) dominated by instinct, fear, and power. The depiction of racism, anti-semitism, and class antagonisms, along with the Fascist materials, did indeed constitute an ambiguous warning, one that was to become more appropriate in Germany as old Nazis re-entered public life.

James Jones's *From Here to Eternity*, which followed *The Naked and the Dead* into print a few years later (1951), was admired by Mailer and shared several features with the earlier book. The action of the narrative takes place in peacetime Hawaii during the period leading up to Pearl Harbour so that, as in *The Naked and the Dead* which was set in the Pacific, the crucial *European* conflict is displaced. *From Here to Eternity* was grimly naturalistic, portraying army life in graphic detail from the activities of regimental money-lenders, 'the 20 per cent men', to the contents of waste-bins. It used the military system to reveal the condition of the individual in a technological, bureaucratic society. Finally, it created a milieu in which the main components were physical strength (often brutality), terror, and domination through power, with General Slater articulating the Fascist ideas of Mailer's General Cummings. However, if Jones can only affirm stoicism and the retention of dignity, there is a greater sense of outrage which links *From Here to Eternity* with the social protest fiction of the 1930s. In this *bildungsroman* or educational novel the protagonist Prewitt is Jones's romantic, doomed rebel-hero. He is also an underdog, one of the dispossessed in a book which displays an unusual awareness of working-class and popular culture. Prewitt is both a boxer and a bugler with a love of the blues and a nostalgia for the 'good' movies of the Depression era.

> He had grown up with them, those movies like the very first *Dead End*, like *Winterset*, like *Grapes of Wrath*, like *Dust be my Destiny* and those other movies starring John Garfield and the Lane girls and the on-the-bum and prison pictures starring James Cagney and George Raft and Henry Fonda.[3]

Add to this the references to the Wobblies, Joe Hill, the Harlan County miners' strike, Walt Whitman, Jack London, Upton Sinclair, and Thomas Wolfe, and Jones's novel begins to look potentially educative for Europeans in ways unlikely to receive the approval of American officials.

Drama

Not only novels but plays too presented a multi-faceted perspective of the United States, one which particularly in 1945–6 accommodated some degree of social criticism. *Awake and Sing!*, *Death of a Salesman*, and *A Streetcar Named Desire* in their various ways portrayed a nation of worried, bewildered people in which, as Edward Albee later said, the panaceas do not work much any more. A review by Hans Heinrich in *Berliner Montag* of the stage version of Steinbeck's short novel *Of Mice and Men* commented on 'this kind of America so different from the usual propaganda line of description, a country in which a large part of the population lives in daydreams with no exit'. Similarly, Max Hogel, announcing his production of Tennessee Williams's *The Glass Menagerie* at the Theater am Brunnenhof, Munich in April 1949, said the play was typically American in its 'tyranny, the fear of life, the ant-like restlessness and worry about the daily needs, the devotion and lack of understanding'.[4] The disillusionment, insecurity, unhappiness, and anxiety that characterize the plays of Odets, Miller, and Williams, the sense of a country that has moved from confidence to doubt, were immediately identifiable in post-war Germany. Many Germans, however, would have been happy to take on the problems that came with life on the instalment plan.

Sombre and pessimistic drama formed only part of the theatrical programme established for Germans through Military Government permissions. OMGUS approved the translation of about fifty plays so that between 1946 and 1950 over 8,000 performances of American plays were given in the four occupied zones. The United States was in the best position to control the reintroduction of drama since its zone contained the most famous theatre towns: Munich, Frankfurt, Stuttgart, Wiesbaden, Mannheim, Bremen, Kassel, and (in part) Berlin. In spite of this good fortune more than half the American-sponsored productions were light, escapist works and in no way contributed to the sort of examination of the German past that might come to terms with it. Above all, the Occupation's cultural politics sought to suppress politically engaged theatre of both left and right.

The aim was a conservative bourgeois theatre with socially critical drama eventually avoided or banned in favour of boulevard drama (farce or domestic realism) or ahistorical metaphysics. Thus, the only anti-Fascist American play allowed was Lillian Hellman's *Watch on the Rhine* which did not appear until February 1947, while Clifford Odets' Depression drama *Awake and Sing!* was performed in the previous year. It was condemned in the American press (*New York Herald Tribune*, March 1946) as unsuitable for Germany since it showed a Bronx family living in 'intolerable squalor'. The play's performances, though, were successful with German critics and audiences, the latter finding comfort in Odets' plea for 'teams together' to produce a better society. By November 1947 the plays of both Hellman and Odets were banned in the wake of growing anti-Communism (see the Evarts Memorandum appended to this chapter), and in the same year the decision to allow Arthur Miller's *All My Sons* to be performed in Germany was revoked.

Forms of art and culture in Germany were seen not solely as pure entertainment but as moulders of mass consciousness. The US policy of re-education and denazification was pursued through the media, for although the authorities claimed that Germans

61

would draw their own conclusions from what they read, saw, or listened to, the aim was clearly to sell America and its way of life by showing it from a favourable perspective. Demand for American plays was stimulated through lectures and dramatic readings in America Houses, newspaper articles, radio talks, and personal contacts with German theatre directors. In some cases Theatre Officers took part in productions: for example, Frederick Mellinger produced *Our Town* in Berlin and Bremen. In addition, American dramatists such as Robert Ardrey and Thornton Wilder travelled to Germany for performances of their plays and participated in discussions with members of the public.

American drama, it was believed, was eminently suitable as a tool of re-education. The unspoken assumption was that since the United States was a model democracy, American drama as an aspect of American culture would inevitably promote democratic values. In view of the actual results there is little point in trying to decide whether this crude logic derived from naïveté and complacency or from deliberate cultural imperialism. Certainly the job description for Officers in the Theatre Section referred to support for American drama 'as a reorientational medium for the promulgation of US culture and intellect'. One such officer, Frederick Mellinger, said in a 1947 report: 'The American way of life cannot be taught any better than by the means of American drama.' Others commended the idealism of American plays and their suitability for conveying a pro-American message. Naturally, plays by American writers were welcomed for the same reasons as books, films, and radio programmes. They provided knowledge of modern America, of how its people thought, behaved, and lived. In addition, they were part of the process of restoring to the German theatre international drama which had been withheld from German audiences for twelve years.

The reasons given for drama's re-educative effect remained on a very general level. Slogans were used in place of argument: the American Way of Life, American Democracy, the American Spirit, and so on, and there was no critical questioning or analysis of these rhetorical phrases. 'America' was viewed holistically as a monolith without any qualitative differentiation, although one American officer, Benno Frank, tried to play down the element of nationality, modestly discounting the notion that American plays were better than those of other countries. He merely hoped that they were not inferior. In any case the influence of American drama did not extend to the creation of a particular school of German dramatists.

Theatre Officers, aware that Americans on the whole took little serious interest in politics, adopted the view that American audiences preferred the theatre of 'entertainment' to the theatre of ideas. It was a simple matter, given their prejudices, to transfer this mentality to the German public and to plan their programmes accordingly. Understandably, Germans after the war responded unfavourably to melancholy working-class drama of the late twenties and early thirties and to stage manifestations of misery. German classical drama, which became a national status symbol by 1949, was, at the war's end, compromised by the abuse and manipulation it had undergone at the hands of the Third Reich, and political drama from any source was regarded with suspicion. With German dramatists either still abroad or unable to provide worthy contributions, contemporary drama was at something of a standstill. An exception was Carl Zuckmayer's *The Devil's General*, first performed in Frankfurt in 1947 and a huge success with German audiences, some going wild with enthusiasm. Its appeal was threefold: Fascism was seen as diabolical and therefore irresistible; the depiction in uniform of a good, honourable Luftwaffe general took the curse off Nazism; and one of its messages, eagerly accepted by a war-weary Germany, was that defeat was an essential prelude to national revival.

The way was therefore open for American drama to act as a stimulus on behalf of democratic ideas with the goal of inspiring admiration and imitation. In this context the American Theatre Section had no need to resort to compulsion: the mere presence of the forces engaged in the Occupation ensured a certain amount of indirect pressure. The framework of political power and the licensing system lay behind the acceptance of a regular quota of American plays in the US zone. Resistance to the imposition of 'American drama' as a permanent theatrical presence did emerge. Some German directors insisted that particular works were unsuitable for their audiences claiming that they were too demanding or created major casting problems. Not surprisingly, this sort of resistance came mostly from the conservative nationalist camp.

There were explicit and sound arguments in favour of American plays. Germans were curious to know the cultural materials of other countries, which had been withheld from them for over a decade. 'International drama' became for the German theatre a symbol of the end of Fascist tyranny, a symbol of release and newly won freedom. The culture of the liberators was especially fascinating since the effects of American military power had been fully experienced and the material affluence of the United States was sufficiently recognized. On the American side it was still necessary to counter Third Reich propaganda which had pronounced *Kultur* to be exclusively German and superior to American 'culture', allegedly only a vulgar amalgamation of skyscrapers, cocktails, and jazz. This could be done by demonstrating that a capitalist democracy was capable of generating and sustaining artistic and literary activities.

The actual selection of plays as part of the re-education plan soon established two distinct classes of drama. One, which was approved and encouraged, offered a perspective on America in accordance with the simplistic imagination of many of the Army's cultural officials. The other, unacceptable to the programme, was preoccupied with social and political problems and therefore challenged the vision of a unique ideal United States. Those involved in making choices were aware that the absence of overt political content in drama was a definite advantage. To display Americans as youthful, efficient, optimistic, and commonsensical, and to show the lifestyle in democratic countries as gentle and tolerant was considered more convincing than blatant propaganda. This ideology, posing as the rejection of ideology, functioned as 'harmless' background colour and description, yet patently assisted in the work of re-education. The avoidance of material with a direct social and local relevance in favour of a broader approach implied a concern with international understanding.

It was thought that Germans would learn most easily from the genre of comedy, although the more pragmatic among those involved did realise that whatever the content and style of play, the mere re-opening of the theatres and the enactment of denazification would not lead automatically to the rebirth of democracy. The ironic parallel with the practice of the Third Reich, which had assiduously manipulated light entertainment for ideological ends was, needless to say, overlooked. Among the comedies of American life licensed for performance were two plays by John van Druten, *The Voice of the Turtle* and *I Remember Mama*. The latter appeared to have both universal and national relevance: its title suggested a monument to motherhood but this could be applied more specifically to German women. From a contemporary point of view the message to be inferred was that 'Mother Germany', by becoming as efficient, thrifty, and inventive as the typical 'house-mother', would overcome her current crisis. Taken on a more literal level the image and role of the mother figure might recall the important position promised to German women (and mothers) by the Third Reich's propaganda.

To some observers the play defined itself as an account of the authentic America relatively unknown to most Europeans, a heartland of ordinary people with a strong feeling for independence and personal freedom. Other prominent qualities were a sense of community and an absence of social prejudice. With their good-natured temperaments, their spiritual stability and their self-confidence, van Druten's characters seemed a bright counter-force to the chaos of the modern world. Like Robert Ardrey's *Thunder Rock*, *I Remember Mama* raised the issue of becoming an American, in this instance showing the way the United States in its role as melting-pot was absorbing the flow of immigrants from other lands. Nevertheless the elements of kitsch in the play, its patent naïveté and its sentimentality irritated some critics, who saw it as a rosy middle-class idyll or as one of Uncle Sam's sugar-sweet ideological CARE (Co-operative for American Remittance to Europe) packets stamped 'Made in the USA'.

The Voice of the Turtle was, even more, a perfect comic prototype of the ideology of non-ideology. Apart from an occasional allusion to the war and 'free people' it failed to register any interest in contemporary history. Descriptive terms applied by the critics to this escapist fable included colourful, light-hearted, and charming; awkwardness and innocence were received as characteristically American. The play's plot of chance adventures and its theme of young love and its problems were recognizable as staple components of Hollywood and Broadway. The remedy for hunger, poverty, Fascism, and militarism, it seemed, was a love affair, set in a fairy-tale paradisal world that happens to be a version of the United States in the 1940s. This model includes large expensive apartments with an icebox in the kitchen, well-to-do educated people – the hero, a soldier, has graduated from Princeton – and black maids. Its main social rituals were cocktail parties, gin rummy sessions, visits to the theatre, and frequent meals. Breakfasts consist of coffee, orange juice, and scrambled eggs; dinners are intimate but lavish, 'Oh, we had the most wonderful Vichysoisse, and duck with oranges, salad with a lot of garlic . . . and Crepes Suzettes . . . ' (I, ii).[5] Yet all this is rendered with an air of bourgeois rationality and 'realism' so the overall effect is one of normality, of average everyday existence, albeit with the incorporation of 'life's little ironies'.

This is incidentally also the world or diegesis of the post-war best-selling novel in the USA reflecting the myth of the classless or almost wholly middle-class society and offering a consensual social formation which believes in the success of the individual. Some visitors to *The Voice of the Turtle* detected a different note, a reflection of an uncertain wartime mood, a hint that America was not all material wealth and bliss. However, the great majority established the play's popularity by responding to its apparent universality. To German audiences these well-fed, affluent characters were identifiably human: happy and sad, doubtful and hopeful.

The lives of 'ordinary folks' provided Thornton Wilder with theme and content in *Our Town*, first produced in the United States in 1938. Its values are those of an ideal small town in the years before the First World War (on four dates between 1899 and 1913). Grover's Corners is a community (*Gemeinschaft*), a neighbourly place where the doctor chats to the newspaper boy and the milkman. It is a humanistic democracy in microcosm though one explained, 'managed' however genially by the Stage Manager, a part often played by Wilder himself. Simplified and disinfected, the small town is also uncultured and superficial. 'Things don't change much' there and, mirroring the transcendentalist strain in American culture, the village seeks to avoid the recognition of evil. Its characters who seem neither to question society or to struggle against their own fate are stereotypes to the extent that they collaborate in their reduction to models. The homogenized folksy rhetoric of the play projects the simple facile wisdom of moral aphorisms and, despite references to war and poverty, an untroubled view of human affairs predominates.

Like Wilder's later play *The Skin of Our Teeth*, *Our Town* was produced in a number of German cities in the 1945–6 season and even more productions took place in 1946–7. 'The image of

America presented to Europeans by *Our Town* is pastoral, complacent, coy, charming and entirely unreal', complained Paul Fussell Jr a decade later.[6] Whatever the image presented the play was not universally a triumph; some reviewers found the characters too mundane, too unheroic, while a Military Government report, commenting upon Max Kruger's production at Berlin's Schoneberg Stadt Theater (March 1946) observed that 'the average Berliner, unfamiliar with the setting of an American village, found the stage action difficult to understand'.[7] Nevertheless, 295,000 Germans saw performances in the period up to 1948 (*The Skin of Our Teeth* drew considerably more – 480,000), apart from those who saw the movie version which played in Munich and Berlin. Both plays were widely discussed by critics and audiences and, by and large, were received with enthusiasm. Following Wilder's visits to Germany and his bombastic, optimistic lectures on Democracy and the Common Man in the fifties, pyramids of copies of *Our Town* were offered for sale like commodities in shop windows. An ironic contrast was thus provided between the 'innocent' spiritual world of the performed play and the capitalist marketing and consumption of the printed text.

The psychology of the German reaction is not difficult to understand or describe. Both critics and members of the public welcomed drama with a positive, progressive outlook, drama which would help them to overcome feelings of despair and hopelessness. In addition, the concept of 'our town' is not dissimilar to the German *Heimat*, which, despite the fluctuation of its reputation, has never been wholly rejected by the general public. *Heimat* means homeland, but also connotes a nostalgic attachment to village, landscape, and language. Just as Grover's Corners symbolizes America (its New England atmosphere suggests the origins of the nation), so *Heimat* in modern German cultural history suggested, at a time of rapid modernization and urbanization, that the virtues of the German people resided in the provincial countryside and the small town. A similar belief informed Popular Front culture in the United States in the late thirties. Also folksy and nationalistic, its populist beliefs can be seen in such films as John Ford's *How Green Was My Valley* and Frank Capra's *Mister Deeds Goes to Town*, both of which were shown in Germany after the war.

The Skin of Our Teeth substituted a perpetual suburbia for Grover's Corners but some spectators considered its performance one of the most important cultural events of the period. The meaning and form of the play were debated furiously by academics and students in Göttingen in 1947: many agreed with Wilder in finding it joyful and reassuring, while others found its vision of recurrent catastrophe too bleakly pessimistic. Written in 1941 in the United States, *The Skin of Our Teeth* anticipated in a remarkable way the wartime sufferings of Europe and created in advance the spiritual conditions of post-war Germany. First produced by Karl Heinz Stroux in Darmstadt in April 1946, the play spoke directly to the precarious existence of German audiences and transported them, as in a dream, to the world of recent horrors and disasters. The play, Wilder insisted, came alive in times of crisis, especially

> in Germany soon after the war, in the shattered churches and beer halls that were serving as theatres, with audiences whose prices of admission meant the loss of a meal and for whom it was of absorbing interest that there was a 'recipe for grass soup that did not cause the diarrhoea'.[8]

Revived in 1952 and 1953, the play continued to make an impression, with some asserting that its meaning was more relevant than in 1946. Perhaps disasters and mere survival were all for the best: Zero Hour did ultimately lead to the economic miracle.

The first American work to be performed in post-war Germany (November 1945) was Robert Ardrey's *Thunder Rock*, a play, in its author's words, for 'desperate people'. The 'actors' for this first production were liberated inmates from concentration camps and the set was made from the rubble that filled the streets of Berlin. Its popularity lay in the development of the leading character and his transformation from cynical pessimist escaping from contemporary society to responsible optimist prepared to play his part in shaping the future. All this was of clear significance to German spectators in 1945, although the play was written before the war. For Charleston the protagonist, humankind's future could be excavated from the past, specifically the pioneer past of an America to be perceived not only as a sanctuary for fugitives but more boldly as a land of opportunity and freedom. The result of his dialectical discussion with the ghosts of dead immigrants is an optimistic belief in progress. The effect is somewhat deterministic and not much is said about the actual role of man/womankind in the historical process. However, Ardrey calls on idealistic people in all walks of life to endure and fight on with a real hope of victory: 'Sooner or later, tomorrow or in a thousand years, mankind finds an answer.' (III)

General critical response to *Thunder Rock* was favourable since it appeared to confront the scepticism and pessimism of Sartre and Anouilh on the German stage. Its message was even taken as an invitation to emigrate. At least in the United States hope was apparently abundant in its democratic society:

Charleston. See America, your adopted land, where the poor go to school with the rich. See women sitting in the House of Commons and in the Senate of the United States. (III)[9]

The message of Ardrey, who worked for the English feature desk at the Voice of America towards the end of the war, repeated that emphasis on courage, fortitude, and stoic resignation found in other writers of the thirties such as Hemingway, Dos Passos, and Fitzgerald. The protagonist cannot make affirmations beyond a vague mixture of nationalism and nostalgia. More important for German audiences was the statement that it is worthwhile to live, work, and participate in society even when the results, in a changing restless environment, are not immediately visible.

Despite the onset of the Cold War, *Thunder Rock* was retained by the Theatre Section in its canon of plays although as an example of progressive drama it soon became a very isolated work. Reference to the Cold War prompts the observation that the post-war years should not be regarded as a single and homogeneous whole. The first two years (1945–6) constituted a relatively free and open time for the theatre, with the American authorities at least allowing, if not actually promoting, liberal plays. As late as 1948 the theatre programmes of the American and Russian zones still showed some similarities. However, the second period (1947–9) is marked by militant anti-Communism and a conscious attack on anti-Fascist theatre. The results for American drama in Germany are powerfully described in the memo by John Evarts (1949), appended to this chapter.

Following the decline of interest in denazification by the Americans (the death of the project being announced officially to the

Counter-Intelligence Corps on 1 June 1948), former Nazis were exculpated and accepted while anti-Nazis fell under suspicion. Correspondingly, the assault on anti-Fascist theatre was being encouraged by the Cold Warriors of German criticism in 1947. By that year dramatists who emphasized social contradictions in the United States were being frowned upon while those who provided escapist or existential plays were supported. Marxist writing was of course forbidden. The 'freedom of expression' rhetoric of *Neue Zeitung* and the reality of the situation were patently at odds. Furthermore, the American claim that the Negro question was a purely American problem was a disturbing echo of Nazi assertions that the Third Reich's policies and conflicts were solely the affair of Germany.

During the period between 1945 and 1949 a whole generation of directors and theatrical workers sympathetic to the cultural policy of the United States was introduced. In addition to romance, escapist comedy and farce (*Three Men on a Horse*, the Broadway success of the 1930s, by George Abbott and John Cecil Holm, was as popular with audiences as *Thunder Rock*), they produced both European and American examples of pessimistic metaphysics which substituted myth and religion for history. Wilder's *Our Town*, the epitome of 'Magic Realism', O'Neill's *Mourning Becomes Electra*, Rice's *The Adding Machine*, and the religious plays of Emmet Lavery had their counterparts in the works of Camus, Giraudoux, Anouilh, Mauriac, T.S. Eliot, and Christopher Fry. The dominance of these aesthetic models thwarted a rational investigation of post-war material and spiritual problems, deflecting or simply ignoring contemporary issues. Their influence upon West German theatre extended well into the 1950s.

The Evarts Memorandum

Bad Nauheim, Germany
4 May 1949

SUBJECT: Control of American Plays
TO: Colonel MacMahon

1. Through the CAD [Civil Affairs Division] a control is maintained over the release of American plays in the U.S. Zone of Germany, and practice has shown that plays in the following two categories are often prohibited from being released and distributed:

a. Plays which tend to contain an element of criticism of life in America, or deal with the major problems facing America.

b. Plays, *regardless of content*, written by authors who are considered to be either communist, or communist-sympathizers.

2. Practically, this results in the prohibition of a good proportion of the best serious plays written in America, either from one cause or from the other. For example, Arthur Miller's prize winning play "All My Sons", falls under both categories; "Deep Are The Roots" under the former; all of Lillian Hellman and Clifford Odets under the latter.

3. Therefore, with some notable exceptions, the American plays available to German producers tend to be lighter comedies, good in themselves, but not the best in the American theatre. And the best plays and authors are not represented – a situation strangely parallel to Nazi times when there were also many forbidden authors. One can see an ironic situation where, just as after the war Nazi forbidden plays were produced all over Germany as a reaction against restriction, American forbidden plays will be produced for the same reason, when control is finally ended.

4. Moreover, German producers, and critics, and all interested in the theatre, know about these good plays which, for one reason or another are not released; they either read of their international

success, or they see them in neighbouring countries, such as Switzerland, or Belgium. And they know that much of the best American Theatre (the one literary front on which the U.S. is currently ahead of other nations) is kept from them by a governmental agency.

5. Furthermore, occasionally the Soviet authorities either legally or piratically get the rights to one of these controversial plays, and sponsor its production in their Zone of Germany, or Sector of Berlin, taking full advantage of the fact that it may be a play critical of America, and withheld by American Authorities. And these productions tend to distort the plays into downright anti-American vehicles. Witness the Russian Zone productions of "Deep are the Roots" and "All My Sons" (the latter now in rehearsal in the Russian Sector of Berlin) – both of which would have been much better produced in theatres in the American Sector or Zone, where they were eagerly sought.

6. The vital point is that such control or censorship is in itself bad – and far outdoes the harm which any selfcriticism exhibited in these plays would do, were they freely presented to the German producers, to be used or not according to their theatrical merits. It is unfortunate that we stand with the Soviets as the only two nations which so control the production of plays in occupied territories.

JOHN EVARTS
Chief, Theatre and Music Section

Chapter six

Magazines: Fantasy Unlimited

During the 1940s national magazines in the United States achieved an enviable position in relation to other branches of the media. The halcyon years of the daily newspaper were over and television was in its infancy. So the dissemination of news and, more importantly, the moulding of public opinion were dominated by radio and by the news and pictorial magazines to which advertisers now made reference, labelling their products 'as advertised in X'. In keeping with their anti-isolationist beliefs, the magazines *Time* and *Life* published international editions 'bringing the products of democratic journalism and the products of the democratic way of life to the peoples of other lands' (*Life*, 9 December 1946). *Time*, which like *Newsweek* sent special overseas editions to the troops, actually planned a German language edition, provisionally entitled *Umlaut*, but no agreement could be reached with the Office of War Information and the US military authorities. Translating *Time*'s notorious style was also a formidable obstacle, so the project was abandoned in 1944. *Life*'s international edition was launched in July 1946 and was a modification of its armed forces edition, first produced in 1943. Its most significant change was the inclusion of advertising aimed at foreign audiences.

German language newspapers and magazines were rapidly set up by the Allies in 1945, the first in the American zone being the *Frankfurter Rundschau* at the end of July. Long queues at printing shops ensured that they were quickly sold out. Although the number of licensed newspapers and magazines grew steadily, newsprint was restricted until June 1948 and rare copies of *Time*, *Life*, and the *New York Times* were swiftly grabbed and read. These copies were scarce, since for some years after the cessation of hostilities it was forbidden to mail books and periodicals from the United States to addresses in Germany. However, by 1946, *Time*, *Life*, *Collier's*, *Esquire*, *Reader's Digest*, *The New Yorker*, and *Free World* (*sic*) could all be found in American libraries there. The United States Information Agency (USIA) put out more than fifty magazines abroad after the war as well as distributing unsold copies of magazines printed outside the USA. Articles from more liberal sources, such as *Politics* and *Partisan Review*, became available in typewritten translations by early 1947. In Washington, DC at the end of the war, however, liberal journals such as *The Nation* and *PM* were considered unsuitable for captured German generals who were restricted to *Life* and *Reader's Digest*. The demand for information was strong and growing: an OMGUS survey in February 1947 of 'overt' American controlled periodicals such as *Heute* or *Neue Auslese* found that the improvement most often suggested by German readers was the provision of more articles on life and conditions in the United States.

Such articles with accompanying images filled the pages of *Time* and *Life* whose influence abroad was immense. The very boldness of their stark yet grandiose titles implied an appropriation by a single American corporation and therefore by the United States itself of the modern world and human destiny, an appropriation for which American power and productivity offered some justification. However, *Life*, America's first pictorial magazine, needed the assistance of a German expert, Kurt Korff, to bring about its successful birth. Henry Luce used its pages in 1941 to announce the emergence of 'the American Century'; a year later OWI claimed that the United States represented the only ideology to which 'men of freedom and good will' could turn. Accompanying the visual and verbal depiction of America in the second half of the forties there was, in various degrees of explicitness, a statement of the democratic mission. Together they gave the impression that the future of the world lay in its Americanization, a view supplemented by wartime propaganda in which the USA appeared as a mighty and benevolent nation with the best interests of the world at heart.

Time–Life's vision of the United States was filled with successful men, beautiful women, new cars, luxurious homes, and large civic buildings. A sufficient number of decent, folksy individuals and families are in attendance to show that this material paradise is available to the common man and woman. In Norman Rockwell's *Saturday Evening Post* cover 'The New Television Set' (5 November 1949) an old man watches with delight from his modest 'granny' apartment as a mechanic places the TV aerial in position. Images that proclaimed America's modernity and power constituted a fabulous dream for the wretched and deprived of a devastated Europe. 'At night across the Atlantic, the great cities of America blazed like modern cathedrals of providence, warm with human kindness and golden optimistic light, full of a dynamic and strong people who were untouched by despair.'[1]

Those qualities, optimism and dynamism, were very much to the fore in a particular venture of the Luce empire towards the end of the decade. *The New America* was a panoramic entertainment made possible by a multi-camera multi-slide system that was a precursor of Cinerama. The emphasis in the presentation was not only on the splendour of the American landscape but also on the nation's dramatic expansion since 1945, which took the form of new factories and schools, prosperous suburbs, and modern shopping centres. The show toured the United States for two years and at the Army's request was translated, revised, and shown extensively in several foreign locations, including Germany.

In *Time* and *Life* a receptivity towards news items and images resulted in what has been described as an indiscriminate but homogenized version of culture available 'democratically' to rich and poor alike. Through the overlay of ideology and national myth, the contradictions of culture are smoothed out. Up to the mid-fifties *Life* spent $25 million on its coloured reproductions of great works of art, but nine pages of Renoirs, followed by a photo of a roller-skating horse, demonstrate the process by which an apparent heterogeneity is reduced to a structure of sequential attractions for the general consumer. By the 1950s Heinz Abosch could make the following comment on similar glossy German magazines:

> Everything is dealt with: from Eden Roc to Soutine, from holidays in Florida to Kandinsky, the latest royal marriage to Brancusi – all treated with the same mixture of frivolity and false sophistication, without the least sense of transition from one subject to the other.[2]

The process also incorporates advertisements which have a fixed relationship with the rest of the magazine. They publicize the consumer goods which have created the affluent society and whose continued production and sale are necessary to sustain it. Thus, for example, when *Life* arranged a 'Round Table on Modern Art' for its 11 October 1948 issue, the reproductions of Picasso, Matisse, Dali, and the Americans, Gottlieb, de Kooning, and Pollock were sandwiched between a full-page advert for the Bendix washing-machine and a double-page spread for Ritz crackers. Not far away could be found adverts for Black and White whisky, Pall Mall cigarettes, Peter Pan Merry-Go-Round bras, and Gaines Meal dog food. Yet magazines such as *Time* and *Life* are themselves, just as much as Coca-Cola or streamlining, advertisements for the American Way. In a revealing statement, Edward K. Thompson, the assistant managing editor of *Time*, said in 1946, 'We know some of the things we want to plug – better homes, movies, books and in general better ways to use leisure.' Admitting that their approach would become direct even brash, he added, 'our technique has something in common with display advertizing'.[3]

The wartime period was a revolutionary one for the advertising industry with the conflict itself becoming a test of the American system, past, present and future. Soldiers could discover through magazine adverts that they were fighting to preserve the corner drugstore, chocolate malteds, Mom's fruit pies, and a dog called Shucks. Tableaux of American pastoral pervaded media culture from about 1943 onwards, repeating rural and regional images associated with Currier and Ives lithographs and Norman Rockwell illustrations: the band concert on a summer evening, the one-room schoolhouse, the newly painted church on a hill. Rockwell's nostalgic painting *Shuffleton's Barber Shop* (*Saturday Evening Post*, 29 April 1950) features three elderly men making music in the back room. In the shop itself the artist has placed the paraphernalia of the barber's trade in addition to kids' comics on a display rack and a cheery pot-bellied stove. The faded Second World War poster is part of the nostalgia; it is also a reminder of the human cost of defending the ethos of 'Smalltown USA'. Those same soldiers mentioned above would also read in the same magazines that the American peacetime goal was a streamlined utopian world, a future of glass cities, superhighways, teardrop cars, and a helicopter in every garage. This 'brave new world', predicated on wartime experiments and discoveries, would replace the bleak Depression conditions of recent memory.

This double thrust (whatever the possible contradictions) gave the advertisers the means of a clear and direct campaign. Both conceptions were suffused by a belief in American ideology and values. 'Freedom' was a key word signifying an absence of regimentation and bureaucracy, but also carrying with it the implication of hostility towards a caring welfare state. Another term central to the American Dream was 'opportunity', the chance to share in the 'good life' of material wealth which free enterprise would provide once the war was over. No wonder B.P. Geyer, the owner of an advertising agency forecast in *Printers' Ink* in 1943 that the tyranny of the Axis powers *and* the New Deal would come to an end in 1944. Conservative thinking of this kind inevitably influenced editorial opinions and policies. Fired by its visionary Americanism which made consumption a patriotic duty, advertising became both more aggressive and more sophisticated, with the employment of mass persuasion techniques for the promotion of corporate images and the marketing of goods. 'Postwar . . . advertising would have a pitch verve and dynamism utterly lacking in the mercantile voice of the 1930s and it would speak with greater force and clarity to the inner self of the media audience.'[4] By the end of the forties Europe, including Germany, would constitute an increasingly significant part of that media audience.

Neither *Time* nor *Life* reported regularly on Germany though each contributed one or more 'progress reports' on the Occupation, *Life* in March 1947 and *Time* later in the same year (May and November). *Time*, like the licensed press, often provided unattractive descriptions of the inhabitants of post-war Germany, describing them as 'insolent', 'bitter', 'cynical', and 'self-centred to the point of smugness'. Ironically the element of spiritual fatigue, of dazed numbness observed by visitors to Germany at this time was also detected by the German film critic Siegfried Kracauer in *Crossfire* and other Hollywood movies about returning GIs. Inevitably black marketeers were featured as the most visible evidence of a widespread amorality: Germans, it was said, were inclined to greet each other with the phrase, *Was schiebst du heute*? (What are you wangling today?). *Time*'s inventory of civilian survivors included long-haired German prisoners of war with cigarette butts trailing from their lips, restless militaristic youths, old-fashioned bureaucrats, and unreconstructed Nazis. All were seen as ungrateful recipients of food parcels from the people and especially the children of the USA.[5]

Time, along with *Reader's Digest*, in which Max Eastman's attack, 'We Must Face the Facts About Russia' appeared as early as July 1943, was in the vanguard of the verbal Cold War, so that although Germany was a burden, its inhabitants conveniently and irresponsibly amnesiac and showing little or no interest in or compassion for the rest of Europe, its strategic importance was recognized as enormous. In November 1947 *Time*'s correspondent Sam Welles expressed a concern shared at the highest levels of the military and the government: 'If Germany does not get some . . . U.S. aid, chaos and then Communism are almost sure to follow.'

Life magazine also arrived at the perception of Germany as an outpost of democracy, spearhead of the fight against Communism (Editorial, 5 January 1948), but its energies were usually dedicated to creating thrilling and attractive images of the United States. In this it was performing one of the basic functions of American popular culture. One of its early post-war issues displayed farm machinery (harvesters, automated tractors, *all priced*) that would, *Life* assumed, initiate a new era of abundance for the entire planet. That abundance, already achieved in certain parts of America, was made powerfully visible later in the year (1946) in *Life*'s survey of the nation, printed as usual on oversized paper. A 7-year old child is shown dwarfed by 2,500 bushels of his father's bumper corn crop on a farm in Illinois. By 1948 the growth of the American economy had become a phenomenon of such proportions that there were insufficient seagoing ships in the world to transport the goods produced weekly by American factories. The size and expansion of multinational corporations is suggested in resonant language by magazine writers: industry is developing 'new frontiers' and Dow Chemical is said to have created a 2,500-acre 'wonderland' by the sea at Freeport, Texas. The implications of corporate power, which President Roosevelt had already recognized as greater than the government's, are ignored in favour of Big Business as Disneyland.

In that 1946 survey and in similar features, *Life*'s mythical America like that of the advertisers is essentially rural, with the Midwest (especially Illinois, Nebraska, and Wisconsin) still regarded as the centre of America spiritually as well as geographically. Virtue is sought and found in the small town ('The Good

Life in Madison, Wisconsin'), an idealization popularized in the movies of Frank Capra such as *Mr Deeds Goes To Town*, one the Hollywood films allowed into Germany after the war. *Life*'s description of Roary Hammes, automobile salesman turned successful businessman and entrepreneur, might apply to Longfellow Deeds or Jefferson Smith: 'He has a simple, homey ideal of service . . . to his community.' (*Life*, 14 October 1946, p. 10) Even the magazine's report of progress in an American city took for its example Omaha, Nebraska, whose population, as late as 1960, would only reach 300,000, the population of Toledo, Ohio in 1948, and for the *Saturday Evening Post* in that year, 'exactly the best size for good living.'

As a mass market journal, *Life* dealt in simplifications and stereotypes. An instance of mass culture itself, it adopted a perspective on American culture that stressed the popular and the youth-orientated: jeeps, trailer-camps, comic books, zoot suits, jitterbugging, and, in a 1947 feature on the sons and daughters of Army personnel at 'Heidelberg High', jeans, milkshakes, and juke-boxes. These young people may 'try out' German clothes but they 'cling' to American customs in the same manner as the GI colonies in Berlin and Frankfurt with their baseball and bingo games, their steaks and Cokes, their 'Stateside Stomps' in the base's ballroom. The insularity of these groups helped to ensure that eventually their colourful commercial culture was proposed as a package, especially alluring to a Germany (and Europe) bewildered by poverty, uncertainty, social dislocation, and a cultural vacuum. It was a package whose materialistic nature was sometimes paraded blatantly and without embarrassment, as in *Life*'s posed picture of consumer items (dishwasher, power mower, TV/radio/record player, etc.) entitled 'Dreams of 1946'.

If *Life*'s interpretation of America in 1946 and its forecast for the decade to come still seem excessively idealized and optimistic, they nevertheless reflected one facet of contemporary national consciousness. The major film of the year, a winner of seven Academy Awards and a big success at the box office, was William Wyler's *The Best Years of Our Lives*. Harold Russell, the disabled Navy veteran who played an important role in the movie later reminisced, 'But the important thing is that the postwar years *were* a great period for our country, and you had a tremendous feeling just being alive.' (original emphasis).[6] Pride in the achievements of the United States and confidence in the future, allied with the sense of a crusading destiny, encouraged *Life* to interpret modern America as a model society, democratic and multi-ethnic. The impression of an immigrant prospectus becomes more marked when readers are told that 75 nationalities live and work in New York City, and that 'school children of many races and countries learn to be Americans' (3 March 1947). Many of *Life*'s superb photographers, who combined an authentic expressionism with an affectionate semi-sentimental feeling for America, were themselves refugees from Central Europe.

Ideological terms in *Life* and similar magazines (success, democracy, dream) are sprinkled among the visual artefacts to which they are related, but by 1949 the term 'democracy' is also used to articulate current anxieties.

> The dark underside of the shining coin of German economic progress is the West's failure to sell *democracy* to the broad mass of the German people . . . During the occupation, they have known all of the slogans but very little of the experience of *democracy*.[7] (my emphasis)

Life regarded the arrogance still to be found among Germans as undemocratic behaviour, but it is more likely that this criticism, despite the recent lifting of the Berlin blockade, reflects the unease and tension emanating from the Cold War and worry over economic problems in the United States. Comments of this kind are a useful reminder of the contradictions within a culture and in the ideology by which it is suffused: the 'Good Life' in Madison, Wisconsin is compromised by polluted lakes, traffic jams, and increasing urban congestion (27 September 1948). In addition, families are becoming smaller, atomized, their old functions challenged (16 August 1948). Even the New Frontier rhetoric of *Life*'s 1946 anniversary issue was modified by the recognition of youth and labour as 'danger spots'.

Nevertheless, the full extent of social unease and distress during that year was never conveyed. Meat shortages, rising prices, strikes in the rubber, oil, textile and motor industries, and a subsequent cynicism are ignored, though strikes were examined in the licensed German pictorial magazine *Heute* in 1946. GI problems of re-adjustment, marital discontinuity, and unemployment are barely mentioned. They are prominent in the movie *The Best*

Years of Our Lives but the difficulties of homeless veterans or black GIs are absent in the cosy, suburban world of Boone City. And although the banker Al Stephenson reacts against the grasping materialistic atmosphere of peacetime America, it is his confusion that registers on the screen: 'Last year it was kill Japs; this year it's make money.'[8]

The Best Years of Our Lives was greeted with enthusiasm and admiration in post-war Europe where it was widely distributed; to the pauperized victims of the Second World War, Al Stephenson's bewilderment may have been submerged by the enticing images of affluence and leisure in Middle America: drug stores, night-clubs, juke-boxes, Woolworth's, Coca-Cola billboards, and neon lights. Partly shot on location in Cincinnati, *The Best Years of Our Lives* performed one of the roles consciously adopted by the Military Government's magazines in Germany. Henry Pilgert later set this down in official terms:

> The objectives of these U.S. sponsored and operated publications were two: 1. to take a positive approach in supporting U.S. occupation and foreign policies; and 2. to disseminate accurate political and other information about the United States and other democracies as a means of combatting totalitarianism.[9]

To which might be added – to maintain a mood of passive acquiescence in Germany.

It was to be expected that these licensed German magazines would rely heavily upon American materials for their content. *Amerikanische Rundschau*, for instance, would be modelled on *Harper's Magazine* and would include a selection of tales, essays, and poetry by American authors. They also drew upon American examples for their style and appearance. *Heute* (Today) and *Der Spiegel* were based respectively on *Life* and *Time*. *Neue Auslese* (New Anthology) aimed at an educated, bourgeois audience with its digest of literary pieces from other journals. A joint British and American venture until 1948 when it came solely under US control for two years, it undoubtedly answered an intense need in the years immediately after the war. However, like its American counterpart *Reader's Digest*, it made selections for its consumers and so tended to discourage them from exploring and investigating for themselves.

Der Monat, which first appeared in October 1948 and effectively ceased publication twenty years later, saw itself as 'a forum for an open discussion and debate on the basis of free speech'. While noticing this liberal rhetoric the reader should remember that American liberals also support democratic capitalism and during the Cold War were able to form anti-Communist coalitions with the American right. *Der Monat* was not explicitly a political magazine; it was rather an international journal with a particular interest in modern world literature. The leading Western writers of the day, including Americans, were published either through contributions or extracts, and their latest works were reviewed. Moreover, film, theatre, and the visual arts were regularly discussed. Again, the principals were international figures: Picasso, Sartre, Eisenstein, Barrault.

There was nevertheless a Cold War context discernible in the topic chosen for debate ('The Fate of the West', 'East–West antithesis') and in certain articles on contemporary subjects ('China's tragedy', 'Construction of the air bridge'). A number of the American participants, such as Sidney Hook and James Burnham (and the British–Hungarian, Arthur Koestler) had been Communists in the thirties. Like the editor-in-chief, Melvin J. Lasky, they became, in subsequent decades, militant anti-Communists while subscribing to a belief in 'the end of ideology'. *Der Monat* was based in West Berlin, the location for the first meeting of the Congress for Cultural Freedom in 1950, by which time Berlin had become a symbol of the Cold War and was regarded by the American government as a showcase of 'freedom'. Along with Michael Josselson (an Office of Strategic Services veteran), Lasky secretly collaborated with the Central Intelligence Agency (CIA) in the fifties in order to subsidize the activities of the Congress and the publication of the British magazine *Encounter*, founded in 1953. In its anti-Communism, its broad support for American policy towards Europe, and its allegiance to international modernism in literature (Mann, Eliot, Orwell, Yeats, etc.), *Der Monat* was both a precursor and stable companion of *Encounter*, with which it exchanged articles and contributors. It also demonstrated by its anti-Stalinist liberalism the influence of the American magazine *Partisan Review*, for which Lasky had also on occasions written.

The most prestigious of the overtly American operated magazines was *Die Neue Zeitung*, which first appeared in October 1945

Plate 1 Deliberate mistakes competition in *Coca-Cola Nachrichten* (News), January 1950

Plate 2 Captain Pringle (John Lund) bartering a chocolate cake at the Brandenburg Gate's black market for a mattress – from Wilder's *A Foreign Affair*

Plate 3 Captain Pringle delivers the mattress past the Hollywood censorship limitations on illicit sex to his 'mistress', Erika von Schlütow (Marlene Dietrich) at her demolished house – from Wilder's *A Foreign Affair*

◀**Plate 4** The old order and the new. A GI removes a street sign bearing Hitler's name

▼**Plate 5** At an American club, a German visitor tests attitudes towards fraternization

and survived well into the 1950s. Edited at its inception by the talented writer Hans Habe, elegantly produced by means of the best paper, ink, and photography, distinguished by feuilletons and art features (with a bias towards modernism) and yet reasonably priced, *Die Neue Zeitung* was eagerly looked for during the Occupation. In its first month this voice of the Military Government was criticized for being too German and for including too few items of specifically American news. Readers of *Heute* and *Neue Auslese* made similar criticisms in a 1947 survey, although *Heute* attempted to keep approximately one third of its material American (and a further third international). Following instructions from General McClure, appropriate measures were taken. Articles portraying aspects of American life could not only answer the clamour for information but could function as positive propaganda, while overcoming such resentment towards the United States as existed in Germany. One regular feature was an English language course with a pronounced American flavour. An example from 1947 (no. 258) consists of a short science fiction story about televisual cinema in 1975, and it contains the line, 'We know there isn't any conceivable limit to American inventive genius'. *Die Neue Zeitung* also emphasized the need to create a democratic Germany, especially during the period 1947–9 when, like similar German–American magazines, it adopted an unequivocally anti-Communist line.

The readership of *Heute*, published between 1945 and 1951 at the Munich plant where the Nazis had produced their magazine *Völkischer Beobachter* (National Observer), was more widely based. It was markedly popular with women, Catholics, and, in relation to the readership of *Die Neue Zeitung* and *Der Monat*, the less educated in Germany society. Reaching at its most successful point 750,000 readers, *Heute* was in a position to become an enormously important propaganda instrument and educational medium. Education was provided by translations of modern American fiction (by such authors as Faulkner, Wolfe, Steinbeck, and Anderson), features on American culture (Frank Lloyd Wright, Martha Graham, Koussevitsky and the Boston Symphony Orchestra, and the mythic figures of Paul Bunyan and Johnny Appleseed) and articles on institutions such as the jury system and American political parties.

Educative items could themselves serve a propagandistic purpose, with essays on the federal government or the United States

Constitution implying the benefits of democracy. The features on American culture listed above – and the coverage of an exhibition of American painting at the Tate Gallery – were plainly intended to counteract German scorn and condescension. An article on the history of jazz (25 December 1946) was, as the English language digest of *Heute* broadly hinted, a conscious refutation of the Nazi assertion that jazz was uncouth and degenerate. In addition, articles on CARE (Co-operative for American Remittance to Europe) and CRALOG (Committee of Relief Agencies Licensed to Operate in Germany), and on the restoration of German art treasures were aimed at quashing rumours of American indifference towards Germany past and present.

Occasionally features could focus upon a link between Germany and America such as the observance of Goethe's Bicentennial in Colorado, or the history of Black Mountain College, North Carolina, with its Bauhaus connections. More often *Heute* employed the strategy of *Life* magazine – that is, the celebration of, on the one hand, the American regions with their folksy *Our Town*/high school/drugstore lifestyle and, on the other, modern commercial culture epitomized by fashion, cars, movies, and household gadgets. In one fascinating image the two facets of American ideology come intriguingly together: a photograph of a New England town meeting in Pelham, Massachusetts (*Heute*, no. 28, 15 January 1947, p. 17) reveals, behind the officials conducting the meeting, a mass of crudely lettered local advertisments, erected by plumbers, garage proprietors, and various retailers. Freedom of speech is flanked, or rather circumscribed, by free enterprise. Indeed, many New England town meetings were staged throughout the American zone at the behest of the Military Government, thus acting out OWI propaganda about self-government.

Although *Heute* was a German-language magazine, items were occasionally published in both German and English; notable examples are the carol 'O Little Town of Bethlehem' and Walt Whitman's poem 'I Hear America Singing'. Predictably one of the announced purposes of *Heute* – the correction of false interpretations of the United States – allowed the American language and vernacular to enter German consciousness once more, though English language classes sprang up in Berlin before troops had moved into what became the British and American zones. It was however, another German journal, *Der Spiegel* which became the main channel for Americanisms and garbled terms. In October 1949 'Jazz fans', 'Bebop', 'Glamour girls', and 'Wild West' could all be found in a single article. Later, in the fifties, Hans Magnus Enzensberger, the writer and critic, drew attention in *Der Spiegel* itself to the magazine's *Time*-inspired neologisms.[10] Elvis Presley had been described as 'sextraordinär' because he had transported his listeners 'von Dixieland nach Kinseyland'. Words built up with American prefixes (*exaussenminister*, i.e. ex-foreign minister) took their place alongside these hybrids and straight importations. Nor should it be forgotten that the replacement of 'Aunt-Emma' shops and their products by the 'Supermarkt', full of consumer goods, would gauge the modernization and Americanization of economic and social reality in Germany.

Magazines and newspapers played a major role in cultural imperialism, with the licensing process having unforeseen consequences. When the licence requirement was lifted in 1949 the 'licensed press' retained its position of power, and the newspaper industry of the Federal Republic was to be dominated by a new generation of post-war journalists, editors, and publishers orientated, for the most part, towards the West and the USA.

Chapter seven

Jazz: The Sound of Democracy

Jazz has been one of the most enduring forms of Americanization experienced in modern Germany. The racial or religious characteristics of many practitioners coupled with its distance from classical music made it vulnerable to denunciation by the Nazis when they assumed power in the 1930s. Although the force and spectacle of 'symphonic jazz' as played by Paul Whiteman's Orchestra, for instance, appealed to officials of the Third Reich, and American *Hotplatten* were on sale until the summer of 1941, racial remarks and insults emanated freely from the Nazi press, particularly towards the end of the war. Benny Goodman was labelled 'the Swing-Jew'; Fats Waller was described as 'the American musical clown'.

The economic situation of the German music industry also invited protectionist exclusion, but the cultural and ideological arguments against jazz gained more prominence as part of the propaganda effort. Music which, it was claimed, derived from a Hottentot kraal (in other words, 'nigger jazz') had to be considered a vulgar threat to the pure German soul. Such attacks echoed the assault on jazz (as a Jewish conspiracy to 'Negrotize' American culture) made in 1925 by Henry Ford whose autobiography had just been a best-seller in Germany. Jazz did survive in Europe and when the band leader Kurt Widmann regained his labour permit in 1944 he is reported to have called to a friend, 'The degenerate art has won after all!' German survivors of the war recall listening to records or actually playing swing music during air raids instead of fleeing to the shelters. An art for which people were willing to risk their lives was obviously impossible to eradicate.

The proscription of jazz was circumvented in a number of ways: swing music with 'hot' solos as well as dance tunes became part of the German propaganda industry and could be heard on the radio stations used for that purpose. 'Charlie and his Orchestra', for which the best jazz musicians in Europe were recruited, provided the swing background for parody lyrics directed against Churchill, Roosevelt, and the Allies. In addition, the need to keep up morale meant that German bands at dances and in variety shows were allowed to play a diluted form of swing that was considered sufficiently Aryan and non-American. After the destructive air raids of 1943, clubs, theatres, and cabarets were closed in large numbers and many musicians were drafted into the armed forces: and towards the end of the year the last record of dance music was produced. In Berlin the Lubo D'Orio band continued to play at the Café Leon on the Kurfürstendamm until the beginning of 1945. Other orchestras which still functioned were commanded to play for troops on leave, dishevelled civilians and the victims of bombing. Those performances motivated by defiance or simply by an urge for self-expression were necessarily clandestine affairs and often relied on tip-offs about impending visits from inspectors.

Old jazz records in good condition still existed and recordings of German orchestras made in the early forties reveal their knowledge of arrangements by Benny Goodman and by Bunny Berigan. Fascist Germany, through the Lindstrom Company's Swing Music series, was supplying the rest of Europe with original American jazz – played by non-Americans. New discs like clothes, soap, and food followed the well-used route from the occupied countries to the German black market. As Mike Zwerin has demonstrated labels were replaced in order to deceive the authorities. 'St Louis Blues' became 'La Tristesse de Saint Louis', while in Eastern Bohemia, a rendering of the same tune with lyrics mocking Nazism was entitled 'The Song of Resetová Lhota'. In the context of Nazi antipathy towards the music, swing took on the force of a political statement, nowhere more so than in the occupied nations. Svend Asmussen the Danish jazz violinist has recalled its symbolic importance: 'Every generation listened to it. With young people it was a provocation, particularly against the Germans who were really irritated by this American music.'[1]

In the 1940s German youths resistant to military service and the cult of Hitler openly disaffiliated themselves from the authoritarianism of the Hitler Youth movement (and the League of German Girls) and formed an urban subculture of gangs and clubs. The brightly dressed, nonconformist Edelweiss pirates, located in the Ruhr area and elsewhere in the west, were the working-class voice of dissension. Hiking, cycling, or hitching to weekend meetings in the countryside where they sang new lyrics to commercial hits and protest versions of folk and hiking songs, the pirates were a more political formation than their affluent middle-class counterparts, whose clubs had names such as the Harlem-Klub, the Ohio-Klub, the O-K Gang Klub, and the Cotton Klub. They too presented a distinctive appearance, the girls with heavy make-up, the boys with long hair, Anthony Eden hats, umbrellas, and the long jackets associated with zoot suits. Their cool, languid demeanour was derived from the style of certain British and American film stars. Together these signifiers were an expression of their rejection of official culture.

Like 'Les Petits Swings' or 'Zazous', who sought out forbidden American records in Paris, the *Swing Jugend* – as they were known – listened to jazz music and participated in spontaneous, rhythmic jitterbugging at private parties, in air raid shelters, and at city bars or cafés (such as the Lippman restaurant in Frankfurt) where swing bands were tolerated. Horst Lippman, a teenage jazz fanatic whose father's restaurant is mentioned above, even managed to beat the censorship and mail out a mimeographed newsletter entitled, 'Information For Friends of Modern Dance Music'. The discovery of a copy of the eighth edition in an army locker led to a brief incarceration in jail. However, Lippman survived the war to greet the GIs who liberated Frankfurt.

The orientation of the *Swing Jugend* was patently pro-Western, as some of their brash nicknames (Texas Jack, Alaska Bill) attested. Those from Hamburg and other Hanseatic towns of northern Germany usually came from an anglophile middle- or upper-class background: they enjoyed British bands like those of Jack Hylton, Ambrose, and Nat Gonella, but were sufficiently sophisticated to appreciate the superiority of American artists as well as the stylish and sensuous nature of their performances. Discs of Fats Waller from occupied France were very popular with the Hot Club of Frankfurt. Waller escaped the Nazi ban for a time; some of the authorities were not aware that he was black.

The activities of the young German jazz fan were not only social and cultural. They were central to the existential creation of an identity as an anonymous German writer, interviewed by Dr Fred Ritzel, has explained: 'Everything for us was this world of great longing, Western life, democracy – everything was connected – and connected through jazz.'[2] The reaction of the authorities was predictably hostile. The Security Services referred to the *Swing Jugend*'s interest in 'degenerate' culture and 'sleaziness' (*Lottern*) with contempt: 'Ihr Ideal ist demokratische Freiheit [freedom] und Amerikanische Lässigkeit [casualness].'[3] A Nazi report in August 1942 admitted that the youthful clientele in the inner city bars were

> so plainly opposed to the respectable light music conforming to German taste, and are demanding jazz music, sometimes in no uncertain terms, that the bands are gradually giving in, and the wilder, 'hotter' and more jazzified the music they play, the more unrestrained the applause . . . [4]

However, although the *Swing Jugend* consciously separated themselves from Nazism, they were not necessarily opposed to the war: many remained patriotic by inclination and conviction. They may have had fights with the Hitler Youth, but unlike the Cologne branch of the pirates they did not move from deviance to active resistance, that is, hiding deserters, assaulting Nazis, even killing the chief of the Cologne Gestapo. One representative *Swing Jugend* group, the Rostock Swing Boys band had a pianist, according to Dr Ritzel's report, but it was essentially a club where friends played jazz records and discussed them intelligently. Discreet, careful to avoid being conspicuous, they escaped persecution and managed to create their own closed society, their oasis of peace in a war-ravaged environment. This oasis was not only private but also elitist: The *Swing Jugend* regarded the masses and their comforting narcotic pop music ('Everything's over, everything's past') with disdain. Yet the cocoon of the jazz club was equally a fantasy, equally a way of coping with everyday reality.

After the war some of the jazz enthusiasts, including the Rostock Boys, largely gave up their interest in the music. Its appeal as a forbidden commodity and therefore the basis for a sort of dissension tended to disappear along with the atmosphere and pressures of wartime. When everything was allowed, including broadcasts of the Glenn Miller Orchestra, the Boys' commitment faded and such groups later rationalized their defection by alluding to Adorno, who dismissed jazz as 'the false liquidation of art'. Dr Ritzel also suggests that experiences at the end of the war may have brought home to jazz club members the unreality of their wartime world of swing music. He cites the report of a teenage army messenger besieged in Berlin in 1945:

> On the stage of a cinema Kurt Widmann and George Haentzchel in white tails played, with their band, the wildest hottest jazz imaginable, while in the stalls, lying around between and on seats were soldiers with steel helmets and rifles, wounded soldiers with the mark of death upon them.[5]

Although jazz was officially (and virtually) non-existent in Germany between the end of 1943 and the middle of 1945, it was available to German listeners on Radio Stockholm and by means of broadcasts from the American Armed Forces Network, which continued after the war. In particular, the *'Wehrmacht* Hour' in 1944, featuring the Glenn Miller Orchestra, was a German language programme which, with its vocalist 'Ilse' singing the latest hits in German, made many new converts to American popular music. Moreover, when the Allies entered Luxembourg in 1944, they discovered a cache of old but undamaged swing records (Benny Goodman, Glenn Miller, the Dorsey Brothers) used by the German propaganda machine. They were soon put to work for the Allied cause on Radio Free Luxembourg, which reopened in September of that year. In the 1960s, the cultural analyst Marshall McLuhan would maintain that jazz, by totally involving the listener and cutting across verbal barriers, represented the most creative response to radio.

The first American jeep to enter the village of Petzenhausen near Dachau in April 1945 had the words 'Boogie-Woogie' inscribed on the side. The interest of US soldiers abroad in popular music had been sustained by the transportation of instruments, sheet music, and records, including V-records made by artists for no fee on the optimistic supposition that masters and records would be destroyed when the conflict was over. Understandably, the arrival of Americans in Germany at this time was thought to herald a boom in jazz. Some years later the Berlin magazine *Vier-Viertel* claimed that, in the immediate post-war years, jazz swept over Germany with the impact of a hurricane, and it is certainly the case that, although some members of the older generations regarded jazz as *undeutsch*, its appeal was not limited by age, class, or profession in Germany.

Just a few months after the appearance of the 'Boogie-Woogie' jeep, Rudolf Dunbar, a black journalist from British Guinea, became the first non-German to conduct the Berlin Philharmonic Orchestra since Hitler came to power. On that September evening the loudest cheers were not for the Tschaikovsky 'Pathetique' or for Weber's overture 'Oberon', but for William Grant Still's syncopated jazz composition: 'Afro-American Symphony'. By 1954 the churches in Germany were beginning to organize jazz conferences and seminars, and in the same year the Kurt Edelhagen band, combining jazz with twelve-tone music, appeared at the avant-garde Donaueschingen Music Festival. By 1957 both main German political parties were using jazz concerts in order to win votes: jazz symbolized the energy of the modern urban environment and during the peak years of the Cold War supplied an effective image of American tolerance and freedom.

Yet the progress and establishment of jazz within German popular culture was difficult and protracted. Not only were jazz records as rare and valuable as all commodities, but assistance from foreign jazz clubs (including those in the United States) was not forthcoming. Local authorities had other priorities so that the only regular interest displayed came from individual GIs or from the America Houses where lectures on jazz were sometimes part of the informational programme.

The average American serviceman paid as much or as little attention to jazz as his German counterpart. Moreover, the high percentage of southerners and westerners in the Army of Occupation ensured an audience for country music which was broadcast regularly (as 'hillbilly' or 'cowboy' music) on the Armed Forces Network (AFN). A notable performer on such programmes was Grandpa Jones, who came to Germany in the late forties and formed a group called the Munich Mountaineers. In a poll conducted by AFN in 1945 Roy Acuff emerged as the GIs favourite singer and in 1949 a Grand Ole Opry troupe, including Acuff and the legendary Hank Williams, toured military bases in Germany.

American hit songs and dance music formed a central part of the AFN repertoire and sustained a wide popularity among troops and German civilians. Various American genres of popular music, especially ballads, offered pleasures also obtained from schmaltzy German numbers and *Heimatlieder* (regional songs), thus satisfying a bourgeois longing for the afternoon-tea culture remembered from the days of the Weimar Republic. In 1947 Radio Munich even limited its jazz programmes in favour of *Volksmusik*. Gradually, American rhythms, including those appropriated from other countries such as sambas, rumbas, and tangos, began to make inroads upon the German music scene, the acceptance of South American songs and dance tunes facilitated by the popularity they had enjoyed under the Nazis.

As denazification stumbled towards its eventual disappearance, the hit-makers of the Third Reich whose musical fantasies about the homeland, fate, and miracles had contributed to Goebbels's wartime propaganda were allowed to participate once more in German show business. ('Capri-Fischer' [The Fishermen of Capri], which had been copyrighted in 1943, was revived in 1948 and became a smash hit.) Now for a purely commercial market this time, they packaged the old illusions, sentimental and escapist (epitomized by Zara Leander's 1936 operetta song 'Tied Hands' or her 1944 number 'I know there'll be a miracle some day', sung in the movie *Great Love*). 'Worn out Germany sang unceasingly of senors and senoritas, of Maria from Bahia, a false old-fashioned idyll from a kitsch postcard . . . '[6] In the late forties and early fifties the popularity of waltzes, tangos, and polkas is also explicable as a symptom of the desire for a refined lifestyle and social prestige.

The appreciation of jazz was further hindered by the proliferation of pseudo-jazz in its various forms, not least on the Armed Forces Network. Although AFN played the latest jazz recordings daily, the number of broadcasts was small and the accompanying comments ill-informed and superficial. The separation of jazz from mainstream popular music was made more problematic by swing music, which was itself a product of attempts to turn jazz into a more commercial entertainment. When German bands started up again in 1945 they could only revert to the swing music of the late 1930s. This act of homage was taking place at a time when, with the exception of the Woody Herman and Stan Kenton Orchestras, big band swing in the United States was in embattled retreat as the aggressively uncommercial bebop movement was spectacularly emerging.

However, during those early post-war years in the American zone it was an achievement merely to assemble a jazz group. In the smoky, fetid basement bars of Berlin, diluted swing provided the background for jitterbugging, drinking, and sexual negotiations as an army of *Fräuleins* endeavoured to find partners who would provide food and shelter for a night, a month or longer. Elsewhere, despite the short-lived non-fraternization ban, a number of musicians managed to find work (and therefore all kinds of foodstuffs and unaccustomed luxuries) playing for house bands which entertained in the numerous military clubs. Naturally, the best music was usually heard in the officers' clubs: the new band of Erhard Bauschke, who died in a car accident in October 1945, had played for General Eisenhower and was considered to be a top group in technical terms. These exceptional bands also played for the German public and became popular through the competitive events that were promoted. In Berlin, where over forty jazz bands (including an all-girl combination, 'The Swing Babes') played among the ruins, competitions between East and West took place.

Generally, German big bands between 1945 and 1950 lagged behind their American (and English) counterparts by about ten years. Their performances consisted almost entirely of hit tunes, and they rarely had the opportunity to play or practise a more uncompromising style of jazz. In their case, and especially in the light of their economic and political situation, the imperatives of the market-place were dominant and indeed irresistible. Jazz at this time was a luxury that would not earn enough to make a living. Arrangers moved into the hit or *Schlager* sector, enveloping simple songs in grand pompous orchestrations. Mechanical boogie-woogie rhythms, crude versions of Dixieland, 'modern jazz' embellishments, and the pervasive easy-listening sounds of cocktail bar pianos – all these became features of the middle-of-the-road musical scene.

Small bands composed of amateurs and supported by 'hot clubs' in the large cities were limited in their achievements by taking as their models those artists who were prominent in the revival of New Orleans jazz in the forties. Whatever the merits of Bunk Johnson, George Lewis, and Kid Rena, their imitators produced a raw though cheerful mixture of marching music, ragtime and the jazz styles of the twenties and thirties. In fairness to the German musicians it should be stressed that similar groups, also possessing more energy than skill, appeared in other European countries and on campuses in the United States. Today, swing music such as Glenn Miller's 'American Patrol' can still be found on the juke-boxes of Hamburg bars, but among amateurs it is Dixieland that has retained the greater following in the northern part of what was West Germany and in the former German Democratic Republic. By their sheer numbers and cheapness amateur jazz musicians in West Germany would dominate live performances in the fifties, making life intensely problematic for the professionals who depended on night-club work.

Nevertheless, swing music had, in a fitful manner, sustained a presence throughout the war, at the end of which it was poised for wider exposure and success. In 1947 the Kurt Edelhagen band was expanded and soon became known as the 'Big-Band Number One' in the American zone. Edelhagen, for whom the Hot Club of Frankfurt set up its first recording session at *Hessische Rundfunk* (Radio Hesse), also gained the title of the German Stan Kenton. Nor was Edelhagen's troupe an isolated phenomenon: several bands were constantly trying to reach high artistic standards in jazz performance. Berlin was the leading force in popular music during the Occupation and it was there that the Lubo D'Orio band, mentioned earlier, soon established its reputation playing in the American clubs. With its top-class soloists it became one of the leading swing orchestras in Germany by 1947 and started to make gramophone records. Basing its style on the bands of Woody Herman, Glenn Miller, and Harry James, the Lubo D'Orio versions of 'Skyliner', 'Apple Honey', and 'In The Mood', among others, were eagerly accepted as substitutes for the American originals. 'In The Mood', along with 'Moonlight Serenade' and 'Chattanooga Choo-Choo', was played by the Glenn Miller Orchestra in the Sonja Henie film, *Sun Valley Serenade* (1942). This movie was licensed for exhibition in the Western zones and West Berlin. Doubtless it had an impact on jazz fans and musicians alike. The Miller band also toured Germany in 1945: the high point was a performance for 40,000 GIs in part of the huge Nuremberg Stadium, where the stage was decorated with the coloured cloth previously used for Nazi flags . . .

The International Sweethearts of Rhythm, America's first integrated women's jazz band, also began a year-long tour in 1945. Mainly Afro-American and with a definite 'black' sound, the Sweethearts spent a month playing for General Patton's Seventh Army in Mannheim. Black and white units were seated separately. As one of the trombonists, Helen Jones recalled, they were not the only spectators:

> But there were a lot of Germans that came to hear us too. They were intrigued seeing women musicians and especially a number of black women musicians 'cause they had their own perceptions of black women at the time, due to what Hitler had told them.[7]

Perceptions were also challenged by Dunbar's skilful performance with the Berlin Philharmonic in the same year. One German in the audience turned to his wife in amazement, remarking, 'And I thought they were a decadent race.'

As the opportunities arose, different ways were found of popularizing jazz. First, the 'new' German media treated jazz seriously. In 1945–6 German radio stations broadcast programmes assembled by jazz experts and fans who drew upon their own record collections. The effect in terms of response was considerable, with the result that by the end of the forties it was normal for German stations to put out at least one jazz programme each week; by the early sixties this would rise to between four and six programmes a week. These broadcasts displayed varying degrees of knowledge and subjectivity, but they achieved for jazz a level of recognition comparable to that afforded other musical genres. Radio Munich's 'Midnight in Munich' was started by the Americans in 1945, featuring US Army and German musicians. Later, under German presenters Werner Gotze and Jimmy Jungermann, it became one of the best jazz programmes in Europe. Equally successful was Radio Stuttgart's 'Masters of Jazz', which began in 1948 and within a year was attracting large numbers of listeners, not only in Württemberg and Baden but also in northern spots such as Holstein and Hanover. The flood of sensible questions about the music sent to the station indicated the existence of an informed audience with a genuine interest in jazz. One enquiry, however – 'How can you include Glenn Miller on a jazz programme?' – is a useful reminder of the persistence of the controversy over swing's musical status.[8] In later years Radio Stuttgart's resident orchestra, the Erwin Lehn big band, was accomplished enough to rival the Edelhagen band.

The second significant German contribution to the dissemination of jazz took place in the recording studio. Not until 1948 and 1949 did leading jazz musicians tour Germany, and in the preceding years, enthusiasts had to rely on much-prized ancient records and on newer recordings by German and other European artists. Not until the middle of 1949 did Telefunken (which was linked with Capitol Records of America) bring on to the market new discs by American groups such as the Stan Kenton band.

Previously, the German company Amiga, starting with swing music in 1946, went on to produce a jazz catalogue which featured both established stars and promising new talents. Until the end of the forties and the outbreak of fighting in Korea in 1950, Amiga enjoyed the advantage of being an Eastern zone company that also operated in the West. Meanwhile, in the Western zones Brunswick was in 1947 and 1948 reissuing the wartime output of Belgian, Danish, and Swedish orchestras and publishing new recordings made by German bands. Before 1949 records in the pre-war series derived from American and British Decca matrices were only available in the British zone. In that year, however, it became generally possible to buy the earlier works of Louis Armstrong, Duke Ellington, Jimmy Dorsey, Chick Webb, Jimmie Lunceford, and many others.

The last but by no means least of these influences was the urban Hot Club. Organizations of this type, notably in Leipzig and Frankfurt, the latter soon to become the most active jazz club in Germany, brought together old and new musicians to generate the practice and performance of jazz music. In the beginning the act of simply introducing players to each other and to their audience was an important and memorable ritual. Following the pattern of the American 'jam session' these were among the first genuinely stimulating jazz occasions in post-war Germany, enabling musicians to learn, to compete, and to build their reputations.

A number of such events occurred at the Hot Club of Berlin, from July 1947 onwards, and the All-Star band there soon attracted the attention of the Amiga company. Subsequently, several live recordings of the band were produced. Performances in Berlin reached a climax with Rex Stewart's appearances in July 1948. Stewart's tour was a sensation: not only was he the first top-ranking American jazz musician to play at German locations since the Second World War, but by flying in one of the first airlift planes Stewart instantly became a symbol of the United States and its political and economic support for a beleaguered Berlin. His band, which opened at the *Titania-Palast* with a mixture of Ellington standards and Dixieland numbers, was a makeshift affair of black musicians (some West Indian) recruited in Britain. It did, however, include the alto player Louis Stephenson, who had worked with Benny Carter.

The highlight of the tour was the performance on 9 July (1948) staged by the Hot Club of Berlin, with Stewart and his band as guests. This took place at the *Delphi-Keller*, which had been largely pulverized by Allied bombing and where light was provided by carbide lamps and the candles each guest was asked to bring. Also in that month the American trumpet star completed the historic Hot Club of Berlin recordings for the Amiga label, which, with one exception, were the first to be made by black musicians in Germany since 1927. Seven German jazzmen played on the session, which included a Dixieland tune, 'Muskrat Ramble', a German composition 'Bei Dir War es immer so schön', and a blues which featured Stewart's famous talking trumpet imitating groans and wails: 'Old Woman Blues'. Two numbers were directly the result of Stewart's memorable visit. 'Linden Blues' was inspired by a walk through the ruined Unter den Linden; 'Airlift Stomp' was Stewart's tribute to the pilots defying the Berlin blockade. Not surprisingly, the record company, based as it was in the Soviet sector, altered the title to 'Amiga Stomp'.

Stewart was followed by dozens of well-known American performers, both black and white. US jazz concert packages usually gave more performances in Germany than anywhere else in Europe. Louis Armstrong's concert at Hamburg in 1955 ended in riots, broken chairs, and the liberal use of fire hoses. German excitement and passion was still capable of bearing a political interpretation: during his tour of Germany in 1953 Stan Kenton was told by an exhilarated fan, 'Jazz is not only music but also a way of life.' The 'Voice of America', which had sent out live broadcasts from 52nd Street in wartime, continued to give jazz a prominent position in its transmissions. Fans in the East were appreciative of such programmes and of those by West German stations; the Communist authorities for their part denounced jazz as a component of the Marshall Plan, intended to deaden the minds of the masses. Trips undertaken in the 1950s such as Dizzy Gillespie's government-sponsored tour of the Middle East were explicitly arranged as 'hearts and minds' exercises, designed to counter Communism and promote American ideas of democracy.

Gillespie's radical bebop style, advanced in harmony and improvisation, both a cerebral and an ecstatic music, took some time to gain a foothold in Germany where it had to establish itself in a jazz environment largely dominated by swing and Dixieland. When Americans brought bebop to Berlin just after the war German fans were bewildered. Not until the fifties were bebop records available in Germany and even then they were purchased only by a small elite of *aficionados*. However, articles on bebop began to appear somewhat earlier, first in specialist magazines like *Vier-Viertel* and *Melodie*. Then, in October 1949, *Der Spiegel*, desperate like its readers to keep in touch with the latest cultural developments in the United States, published a formidable article on the subject, quoting Jean-Paul Sartre and comparing the new music to surrealist painting. Several perspectives on bebop as art were advanced, but it is not difficult to perceive here the ideological imperatives that lay behind the Dizzy Gillespie tour of 1956 mentioned above. Bebop, we are informed, is an extension of 'hot' music, one which has 'the *independence* of a *fresh beginning*, the feverish and hectic joy of *free* improvisation' (my emphases).[9]

These are terms encountered in the investigation of other areas of 'democratic' re-education in the American zone. From the authorities' point of view, jazz, particularly in the form of swing music, had proved its usefulness not just as a means of social control but also as a proselytizing agency. Like the plays of John Van Druten, the populist and melodramatic movies supplied by Hollywood, and the middlebrow contents of *Heute* magazine, it was part of the light entertainment invasion of Germany and so participated in the shaping of German mass culture during the period of the American Occupation and subsequently.

Chapter eight

Coca-Cola and Cars: Icons of the American Dream

Coke

In Europe, the United States, and, more recently, the Third World, Coca-Cola has come to symbolize America and American culture: indeed, the identification was already so strong by 1948 that when non-Americans thought of democracy, it was claimed, they instantly called to mind Coca-Cola. As a symbolic artefact it remains powerfully resonant, implying a culture in which certain values and attitudes predominate and in which there is a clear conception of the ideal society.

Although Coca-Cola was invented in the Southern states, it was soon accepted throughout the USA. By 1923 when Robert Woodruff took over as president, it was a national phenomenon, poised for international expansion. Not until 1972 were regional characteristics considered sufficiently acceptable on a national scale for Coca-Cola to use regional images and a country-pop song in its TV advertising.[1] As Helmut Fritz has written:

> From the beginning, Coca-Cola's sales politics were to be present at every showplace of American life: in the supermarket and in the family, at the sports stadium and at the filling station. The gas station is perhaps the most heavily symbolic trade centre for the drink. Coke and gas – the average American can hardly imagine civilization without both these fuels of the American Way of Life.[2]

The modernization of Germany in the thirties, especially the road-building programme, enabled Coca-Cola to feature stream-lined cars in its advertising. In one poster, a motorist is being served a cold Coca-Cola in front of a smart roadside café in the country by a neat young waiter. The tone of the copy is moral and paternalistic: 'Protect yourself from tiredness at the wheel. Refresh yourself regularly.'

After the Second World War, Coca-Cola advertising slogans, such as those on display at the 1948 international conference in Atlantic City, reflected the global growth of the company or, from another perspective, the expansion of American business and Cold War ideology. Among the most relevant examples are: 'Coca-Cola helps show the world the friendliness of American ways', 'As American as Independence Day', and, with a reference to American radio propaganda, 'When you have a Coke listen, listen to the Voice of America.' The term 'Coke' had been used in advertisements since 1941: registered as a trade mark in 1945, it played an important part in post-war publicity for the drink.

Thus, Coca-Cola was visibly in the forefront of American cultural penetration of Europe. Its unique position and symbolic density were quickly recognized by the Eastern Bloc countries, where it was described as narcotic, addictive, and a corrupter of youth. The modernity of Western European societies, manifested by a combination of wealth, technology, and media, had already in the pre-war period made them suitable potential customers. The success of the drink in Germany in the thirties, partly attributable to consistent and extensive advertising through folders, posters, signs, calendars, and slides, was to be repeated in West Germany, which would become the second largest Coca-Cola market after the United States itself.

The production of Coca-Cola in Germany began haltingly in 1929 in Essen, a town already prominent as an industrial centre and therefore one where the thirst of large numbers of workers would need quenching. However, it was not until the dynamic Max Keith took over the enterprise in 1933 that a rapid development of the company took place. It was in the same year that a massive tie-up between Coca-Cola and MGM (beginning with *Dinner at Eight*) was announced through full-page colour advertisements in American magazines. Despite the widespread popularity of beer, sales doubled in that year to 111,000 cases, encouraging the creation of a second plant at Frankfurt in 1934, and by 1939 sales ran to four and a half million cases. One difficulty lay in the attitude of some Nazi officials who were suspicious of the caffeine content. A further reservation surfaced when a rival reproduced photographs of Coca-Cola corks bearing a kosher sign. In the words of *Der Spiegel* years later, 'For the Nazis this foreign drink had too much of a Judeo-American taste.'[3]

By mid-decade, however, advertising for 'this foreign drink' began to reflect the Third Reich mixture of modernity and folksy nationalism, and in 1936 Coca-Cola established itself more securely by providing refreshment at both the Winter (Garmish-Partenkirchen) and Summer (Berlin) Olympics, as it had done in Los Angeles in 1932. Placards and posters for the product showed a mother and child or a film crew enjoying a break, or various sportsmen and women – footballers, cyclists, and swimmers. Both work and play offered occasions for refreshment, but despite the origins in industrial Essen, and consistent with the projecting of a consumer society, there was a bias towards play. Keith shrewdly advertised his product at youth rallies and bicycle races. Clearly, the emphasis on sport, one revived in post-war publicity, was in line with current cultural ideology epitomized by the Berlin Olympics.[4] Moreover, by servicing the Olympics, Coca-Cola associated itself with the modernity of media technology, in the form of microphones, transmitter vans, and cameras for (respectively) radio broadcasts and Leni Riefenstahl's famous film, that was prominent at the Games. Cameras from the USA also provided television pictures for a minority audience. Its promotional activities soon suggested wider horizons. In 1938, a figure with a world map in one hand and a Coca-Cola bottle in the other announced: 'Ja! Coca-Cola hat Weltruf' (Coca-Cola has a world-wide reputation) – a sentiment consistent with Hitler's proposed one-world economy.

Advertising during the years before the war had become increasingly geared to German culture and more independent of American layout and concepts, but not completely. From its inception Coca-Cola had used female celebrities and other attractive women in its posters, trade cards, calendars, and sheet music advertising. 'Nothing is so suggestive of Coca-Cola's own pure deliciousness as the picture of a beautiful, sweet, wholesome, womanly woman', declared one of its American advertisements. In Germany also film stars and models, glamour girls generally, appeared in tasteful 1930s promotional material. Appropriately, pre-war franchisees met in the *Lichtburg*, Germany's largest movie house. The American poses and pictures were vetted by Coca-Cola's president, Robert Woodruff, a pious Southern gentleman, to ensure that they conveyed purity, cleanliness, and an idealized view of women. A task of this kind was unnecessary in the Third Reich where such banal antiseptic virtues were characteristic of female figures in Nazi art of·the period. Later in the 1960s Peter Rühmkorf, in his poem *'Werbe-Beratung'*, (Advertising advice) parodied the Coca-Cola message in an ironic couplet: 'After you've had sex with Lola / Take an ice-cold Coca-Cola.'

The Second World War witnessed an extraordinary phenomenon in the history of marketing and of mass culture. Assisted by an obliging US government, Coca-Cola literally invaded Europe and other parts of the world. 'Technical observers' attached to the armed forces set up entire bottling plants costing as much as £250,000. These were transported to the front lines and moved forward as the American troops advanced. Democracy and patriotism were thus poured down the throats of GIs who drank ten billion bottles during the war at a nickel a time. Since Coca-Cola was by now the principal commercial symbol of a thoroughly propagandized American way of life, it was logical that one of its former advertising managers, Lieutenant Commander Price Gilbert, should, in 1943, be put in charge of a new Bureau of Graphics at the Office of War Information. Henry Pringle, one of those who resigned at the time, responded to the appointment by mocking up a poster in which a Coca-Cola bottle was wrapped in an American flag. The text read: 'Step right up and get your four delicious freedoms. It's a refreshing war.'

In Germany at the beginning of hostilities, however, the raw material situation limited the production of the drink (which stopped altogether in 1942) and advertising was drastically reduced. Peeling posters remained to tantalize GI prisoners of war on forced marches. Ironically, the drink's appeal was now that much greater since its caffeine content made it an acceptable substitute for coffee, which soon became unobtainable. Unfortunately, the last of the syrup from the United States was drying up at Essen during 1940, the year before sugar was rationed. Keith had to turn to the manufacture of a new *Phantasiegetränk* based on lemonade. Appropriately called Fanta, it was to utilize materials available in wartime, and for many housewives it provided yet another substitute, this time for sugar. It was used for sweetening soups and other dishes. Even when machines had to be dug out from the rubble and repaired, and when railway and mail services ceased at the end of the war, Fanta continued to be bottled and delivered. Consequently, the Coca-Cola Company in Germany made money every year during the war. When the Allied victory in Europe was proclaimed, Keith instantly contacted Coca-Cola in Atlanta. His telegram read: 'Coca-Cola GmbH survives. Please send the auditors.'

As the international conflict came to an end, dozens of plants, most financed by the American government, stood ready to take the lead in the commercial exploitation of Europe, Asia, and Africa. This was fitting since Coca-Cola was not only, as Woodruff himself proudly proclaimed, 'the essence of American capitalism', but was also one of the world's earliest multinational corporations, both forming and needing a consumer society. A global corporate economy was encouraged by the State Department and its realization advanced by the Marshall Plan. A combination of expansionist economics and Cold War patriotism characterized the chief executives of Coca-Cola, notably James Farley and Woodruff, the former undertaking a world-wide tour for the corporation as early in the post-war period as 1946. On his return Farley stressed the helplessness of non-American nations and hence their need for American aid and goods. Eventually the 'Mission on the Rhine' would have commercial counterparts and Coca-Cola would look increasingly like a secular religion engaged on a crusade and with slogans substituting for a creed.

Another executive showed more frankness in alluding to the profit motive at the heart of the Coca-Cola empire and associated enterprises: 'Everyone who has anything to do with the drink makes money and becomes a member of the bourgeoisie.'[5] Those destined to remain customers had their own desires and their own reasons for brand loyalty. 'By consuming Coke . . . , the consumer simultaneously buys and consumes the image . . . which carries the promise of happiness, life and belonging rather than misery, death and alienation.'[6] This perception applied particularly to the suffering and deprived of Europe at the end of the Second World War, for whom the promises of the thirties, in Germany at least, were eventually to be repeated.

A survey of the best-known brand-named articles was carried out in parts of Germany in 1947. Coca-Cola was far and away the leader in the alcohol-free refreshments category, although no bottles of the stuff had been on the market for five years. The company had, however, until 1946, sponsored jazz on radio featuring such artists as Count Basie, Duke Ellington, and Artie Shaw. Also on radio the Andrew Sisters could be heard singing 'Rum and Coca-Cola', a 1944 number set in exotic Trinidad with an explicit imperialist context: native mother and daughter are both 'working for the Yankee dollar'. In PXs and other American Army installations, coolers with the famous trademark could be found, and anyone in contact with military personnel had the opportunity to spot and even obtain the drink. German kids got their share from friendly GIs. Wrigley's chewing gum was able to profit from a similar visibility. K-rations were packed in Wrigley's plants so he was allowed to manufacture his product throughout the war. It was at the Army's request that Wrigley supplied a stick of gum in every pack of K-rations.

In addition to the goodwill of consumers, Coca-Cola benefited from the fact that the wily Keith, who transported drinking water for local authorities in wartime, had saved company property from confiscation including the distinctive trucks. Moreover, its well-organized concessionaires, who were already being encouraged to prepare for the future by forming bigger companies, were in a position to be reactivated as soon as the time arrived. This state of readiness was expedited by Coca-Cola in the USA, which began once more to supply the necessary basic materials. The ex-heavyweight boxing champion, Max Schmeling, who was placed in charge of the concessionaires, provided a link with the sporting motif so popular in pre-war Germany. Plants were rebuilt in 1948, employees' homes repaired, and the ingredients started to become available in quantity and quality. Even when Fanta alone was available (in that year) the house magazine continued to use the title *Coca-Cola Nachrichten* (News) and, on the cover, the familiar wide-eyed, happy pageboy with a Coca-Cola cap as headgear. In March 1949, the practice of a different cover for each month was instituted.

The second launch of Coke took place in October 1949. In the previous month Konrad Adenauer had been elected Chancellor of the *Bundesrepublik*, so that the sense of a 'new start' (Keith's own phrase in the house magazine) was shared by company and nation. The past was by no means ignored. *Coca-Cola Nachrichten* reported the celebration of the re-opening with the headline, 'Coca-Cola family party as before', but many of those in the drawing are heading for the celebration in modest but stream-lined cars and coaches. Nor, despite the independence of Coca-Cola GmbH was the provenance of Coke (and the contin-uing presence of occupying troops) avoidable. A deliberate mistakes competition in *Coca-Cola Nachrichten* depicts Germans sampling the drink at a soccer game, but GIs are also in evidence. One US officer (wearing sunglasses on a freezing day) tries to tempt a *Fräulein* with 'Have a Coke, baby!' (see Plate 1, between pages 82 and 83.).

Six factories resumed production in Essen, Hamburg, Frankfurt, Kassel, Stuttgart, and Nuremberg. Rusty signs were rescued from cellars and put to use in advertising; but new slogans inevitably appeared for, as the backs of lorries confiden-tly announced from Day One: 'Coca-Cola ist wieder da!' (Coca-Cola is here again!). With sugar rationing coming to an end in May 1950 Coca-Cola was able to operate at full capacity once more. Nevertheless, some retailers were still unacquainted with the drink and, as in the thirties, the beer lobby was strong enough to eliminate complacency. The aggressive Coke adver-tisement, 'Plagt dich ein Katzenjammer? Eiskaltes Coca-Cola hilft' (Are you bothered by a hangover? Ice-cold Coca-Cola helps) was soon withdrawn by the parent company in Atlanta but showed the willingness of Essen to take on its competitors with no holds barred.

By 1954, when the company celebrated twenty-five years in Germany, there were ninety-six bottling plants operating in West Germany and Berlin. Advertising continued to explore a variety of possibilities, including the large show window where the public could watch the bottling room both day and night. Moreover, the slogan introduced in 1955, 'Mach mal Pause' (Take a break) made such a tremendous impact that it was used for ten years and was registered as a trade mark. Before the war Coca-Cola had used 'Jetzt machen wir Pause', and the use of 'pause' in the marketing of the product goes back in the USA to 1929 and the slogan, 'The pause that refreshes'. Indeed, from the fifties onwards, German advertisements began to use the model of American style and content more frequently. As the Germany of the economic miracle grew to resemble the United States and its affluent society, it was appropriate that the underlying message of some advertising should appear to declare that social redemption now lay not only in work but also in leisure and consumption.

Design at the Centre

By the 1930s Hollywood movies were making familiar to Europeans the details of a contemporary lifestyle and environment, one heavily influenced by modern technology and design. Frank Capra's *Dirigible* (1931), for example, displays in a short early sequence images of a biplane, an automobile, an airship, and a microphone – travel and communication motifs later completed by a radio (with Art Deco housing) and newspapers (available within a day throughout the United States). The iconography of Capra's *It Happened One Night* three years later (telephones, radios, diners, rail and bus stations, planes, and newsreel cameras) is equally rich. The famous hitch-hiking scene provides an inventory of the cars and trucks to be seen on the roads of the United States in the early thirties.

For Europe during the inter-war period and (in some instances) earlier, America held out an entrancing, glamorous vision of affluence, technology, and geometric orderliness, a picture of the future worthy to be compared with the architectural triumphs of the past. Walter Gropius, who was to transport the ideas of the Bauhaus across the Atlantic, claimed that 'the newest work halls of the North American industrial trusts can bear comparison in their monumental power with the buildings of ancient Egypt'.[7] Perhaps the dominant image which epitomized modernity and the American city was the skyscraper made available visually to Europeans through magazine photographs of New York. Indeed, the first issue of *Der Spiegel* in January 1947 was to include just such a picture of New York landmarks.

If the human environment of the future was, in the eyes of Europeans, to be patterned on the typical American cityscape, it would be characterized by clean, smooth lines, regular and mechanistic. In other words it would be streamlined. Neo-classical lines could nevertheless inspire a romantic attitude as some of the German modernists demonstrated: 'In the 1920s [this attitude] spills over from the unexecuted projects of Mies van der Rohe and the illustrated books of Bruno Taut and Eric Mendelsohn into classic movies like *Metropolis* . . .'[8]

Unlike the architects and designers for whom modernity was aesthetic, the engineers (of both the Weimar Republic and the Third Reich) developed an ideology of 'reactionary modernism', as Jeffrey Herf has termed it. This concept combined technology, nationalism (increasingly), and romanticism in the sense of will, blood, instinct, nature, the soil, and the race.

Seen from this specialized and ethnocentric perspective the United States was a soulless anathema, a technocracy in which not engineering but individualism and capitalism were primary. The Soviet Union, on the other hand, through an adherence to materialism and scientism, had produced an abstract, rationalized technology without emotional or cultural significance. Germany, the engineers and theorists announced, would pursue a third way *between* commercialism and materialism; Germany would become 'the land of *Technik* and . . . *Kultur*'.[9]

An emphasis was therefore placed on the spiritual benefits to be derived from the construction of superhighways in the country-side, and when Goebbels made reference to romanticism, impulse, and the soul at the opening of a motor show in 1939, the combination of rhetoric and occasion created a resonant national and cultural paradigm. However, despite the hostility of reactionary modernists to the United States, the coexistence proposed – of *Technik* and *Kultur* – would juxtapose Americanized and *völkisch*, or national, elements within social reality. This contradiction was embodied in Hitler himself and in Porsche's Volkswagen, depicted in magazines as a streamlined machine but one with *Kdf-Wagen* in Gothic script on the number plate. Moreover, several Germans in the motor industry were unequivocally impressed by aspects of the American system. Porsche and his secretary, who made visits to the United States in 1936 and 1937, noticed with approval the extreme cleanliness of American factories and were intrigued by the democratic nature of their cafeterias. Personnel trained in the USA, including executives, were recruited by Volkswagen in the late thirties. Nordhoff, who was to head the revival of Volkswagen after the Second World War, trained not only at the Rüsselsheim plant of Opel (a company bought by General Motors in 1929 at a very low price) but also at Detroit, where his development into an American style industrial manager was facilitated. Volkswagen was to set up a position for a Public Relations Officer as early as the second half of 1946.

During the 1930s 'brown' or Nazi culture was based on an amalgamation of the modern and traditional, of the mechanical and craft-oriented as applied in everyday aesthetics. John Heskett has shown that the styles and forms chosen were already in existence.[10] They were not specific to the regime and were simply taken over by it. This includes manufactured items particularly associated with the Third Reich such as the Volks- (or, as Hitler named it, KdF-) Wagen (Strength through joy automobile) and the *Volksempfänger* (People's receiver) radio, the latter based on a 1928 design. Although Gropius's design for the Adler Cabriolet in 1930 was massive, geometric, and boxy, the use of the circle as a design motif for the Volkswagen looked like a return to Bauhaus principles. However, the model derived its final form from the Chrysler Airflow car of 1934 and the machinery for its production was mostly imported from the USA. It was financed by the savings of 320,000 would-be owners but neither the car, nor the stream-lined technological utopia which, along with Porsche's Auto-Union racing counterpart, it prophesied, became available to either the proletariat or lower middle-class workers. (At the other end of the social scale, racing-car drivers received the same adulation as film stars.) That consumerist vision would only take substantial shape – once again as compensation and promise – a decade later, encouraged by and satisfying the needs of those controlling the commercial and foreign policies of the United States, Germany's erstwhile foe.

The drive towards standardization and the growth and recognition of American norms of consumption and leisure had already become apparent in the Germany of the 1920s. The powerful influence of American commodity culture between the wars, an influence greater than that exercised upon France or Britain, is inescapable despite the announcements and criticisms made by Nazi ideologues. It was a function of the international expansion of American capital after the First World War and was achieved either by investment in Germany industry or by forming part-nerships with German businesses.

By the 1930s the streamlined product style was regarded in the United States as a synonym for modernity. It was a derivation from commercial aviation: after the war Harley Earl's automobile designs would reflect the impression of speed *he* detected in aircraft. 'Finally, even such quiet objects as radios, irons, cash registers or lighters appeared as though at any moment they would race away.'[11] In Europe subsequently, and especially after the Second World War, streamlining was to be the identifiable sign in commodity aesthetics of modernity and of Americanism also.

'American' and 'jazz' (used as an adjective) were treated as interchangeable terms in the discussion of American styles of design between the wars. Later, Edgar Kauffman, in his celebrated essay 'Borax and the Chromium Plated Calf' (1950), pursued a series of analogies between streamlining and jazz. In pointing out that both were highly commercialized and relied on the star system, however, he drew attention to links with another influential area of popular culture: Hollywood. Intellectuals in Europe as well as the members of that consumer society by which they were alarmed or fascinated (often alarmed *and* fascinated) were inclined simply to equate the United States with mass culture. For them too the terms 'America' and 'Americanization' threw up an interrelated range of associations, a multiple stereotyped image of the kind outlined in the special issue of *The Architectural Review* for December 1950, 'Man-Made America': 'Jazz, the movies, Main Street, Highway Culture, teen-age fashions, know-how, framed houses, a language of forceful colloquialisms and a universal literature of whodunits' (p. 416).

With the modernization of first the American zone and then, during the economic miracle, West Germany, Americanism functioned to shape the everyday environment through the impression made by American goods and the prospect of an affluent life-style, inscribed in content, appearance, and brand-name. Now those superhighways of the Third Reich became the sites of numerous fast-food cafeterias with such names as Sunset Inn and Tuxedo Junction. Even the hardship, poverty, and 'gold rush' atmosphere of the late forties, when recollected nostalgically, came to resemble the early history of American towns and industrial enterprises. Many of Germany's 'pioneers' were post-war immigrants, refugees from East Prussia, Silesia, and the Sudetenland in Bohemia.

With the emergence of the Cold War, culture and political rectitude were closely identified so that no serious attempts were made to initiate radical changes in the field of commodity design in the Western zones. To take one example: Braun's 550 electric razor, introduced at the Frankfurt Trade Fair at the end of the forties, was based on a 1938 prototype. Its cautious good taste would in a few years look dated when compared with such models as Remington's 1953 equivalent. The basis of post-war design for those who could afford it was to be the 'Moderne' of the pre-war period. From about the time of the currency reform, then, the period which followed witnessed the creation of a domestic environment of lampshades, baby carriages, kidney-shaped tables (and some resembling boomerangs or palettes), espresso machines, and cars, one which sought its coherence from American variations of streamlining. The imitative demands of kitsch were met by the use of plastics and other synthetics in the form of butterfly glasses (with false eyelashes!) and radios enclosed in leatherette.

Moreover, as in the case of any other design concept in the United States, the demands of the market and of popular taste came first. The leading designers of the post-Depression period, such as Norman Bel Geddes and Walter Dorwin Teague, had run their own freelance offices on a commercial basis, corresponding naturally to an industrial world preoccupied with sales, profits, and corporate identity. Like the commodity culture of Germany under the Nazi government, streamlining was far from being the manifestation of aesthetics in a vacuum. A sense of mission, of planning a more perfect society, was present, but Raymond Loewy succinctly expressed the essence of the American strain: industrial design delivers the goods.

Streamlining remained offensive to a European establishment which held that good design should be tastefully restrained and which labelled the Americanized style decadent and decorative. (Automobiles of the forties provoked a similar but more sophisticated German assessment contained in the phrase 'Detroit Machiavellismus'.) However, it did have the advantage of what has been called 'an expressive design vocabulary', one not necessarily related to the product it enclosed.

Despite Siegfried Giedion's reservations published in *Mechanization Takes Command* (1948), the visual assertiveness of 'styling' was part of its very attractiveness to certain Europeans who came to realize that banal American objects such as the Coca-Cola bottle were often the most consciously and most conspicuously designed.[12] The development of the Coke bottle (the shape, the white lettering) by Raymond Loewy and his 'white' packaging of Lucky Strike cigarettes, originally green, are instances of the way American industrial designers created the environmental imagery that filled the urban spaces of Europe after the war.[13] Loewy, who also designed the new streamlined drinks-cooler and dispenser for the Dole Company in 1947, aimed for a 'very high index of visual memory retention'. The best example of this is found in Lucky Strike, where he put the trade mark on *both* sides of the packet. It was Loewy who came up with the concept of MAYA (Much Advanced Yet Acceptable), which mirrored Hollywood's combination of the standardized and the innovative.

A significant example of the styling referred to above was the new five mark note in 1949 just after the creation of the Federal Republic. On the right of the bill was depicted Europa riding a bull, presumably towards the utopia of the economic miracle. A further traditional element lay in the Gothic script stating the note's value. Behind and beside this appeared a design in the form of an undulating web or network described by critics as a jumble of lines in the manner of Picasso. The pattern derived, of course, from streamlining and thus linked the ancient myth and lettering with an image of 'the modern'.

In post-war Europe as in the United States, the appeal of the streamlined continued to be based upon 'newness' and 'scientific progress' – literally the shape of the future. An American future with the vision of a new American era filled with smooth glossy consumer goods carried a special meaning for those in Europe suffering acute penury and hardship.[14] The traffic was by no means one-way (especially after 1949). The Reynolds lightweight aluminium pen was phenomenally successful in the United States in 1945: ironically it had originally been made in Germany.

Plastic had also been promoted as the image of the future when, in the late thirties, it had shown itself a suitable medium for streamlining; after the war it was still associated with the 'Moderne' because rounded and sculptured contours could make glossy plastic look glamorous. The expansion of the industry during the Second World War was encouraged so that scarce metal could be freed for military purposes. The GI with his vinyl raincoat, melamine dishes, and cellulose canteen helped to introduce synthetic materials into Europe. Eventually, if only on the level of 'damp cloth utopianism', plastics (in floor coverings and domestic decorations) became for Germans and others part of a modern environment in the American style. The resumption of the production of synthetic fibre (*Glanzstoff*) took place in Germany between 1945 and 1947, leading in 1950 to the introduction of Perlon. In the United States, however, as a result of products snapping, dissolving, or going out of shape, the image of plastic was often ambiguous despite the optimism of magazine writers. By the end of the war a significant section of the public was demanding 'genuine' materials once again.

Plastics made a convenient weapon with which to criticize American life as shallow, materialistic, and vulgar. Even Raymond Loewy later noticed how America (and by implication Europe) became flooded with inferior gimcrack products rendered seductive by an 'advanced' futuristic appearance. Generally, however, industrial designers had been persistently enthusiastic in their writings and statements. Teague in particular acted as a booster for the new technocratic society of mass consumption. *Life*'s two-page spread, advertising the latest out of Detroit, might represent affluence, but Loewy, planning the post-war Studebaker, also insisted, 'The car must look fast whether in motion or stationary' and streamlining provided that enticing metaphor of movement. Standardized technology implied modern democracy while speed and mobility, especially in the American context, were part of a vision of freedom.

However, one of the most enduring images of the American Occupation had less to do with speed than with effectiveness and reliability: the ubiquitous Willys Jeep. Following the war it was used not only for military purposes in Germany but also for transporting the mail and distributing water to refugees. It also doubled as an ambulance. Later, in Austria, farmers, firefighters, and soldiers all came to rely upon its ability to handle rugged terrain and mountain paths. In the fifties thousands of Auto Union Mungas were produced for the *Bundeswehr*, NATO, and German civilians. It resembled the boxy jeep much more than its rivals from the Porsche and Goliath companies. That the jeep was seen as an instrument of Americanization is demonstrated by the OWI film, *Autobiography of a Jeep* (1943), made in sixteen different languages and one of the first films to be shown in Frankfurt after the Second World War. This documentary presented the USA as a land of high-speed cars and modern highways as well as stressing its large-scale industrial machinery. A Disney-like instinct made the jeep into a first person narrator with democratic beliefs: despite being photographed with both

Roosevelt and King George VI, it is 'my pal the soldier' who matters most.

By the middle of 1947 *Der Spiegel* was starting to publish photographs of new American cars. The 'Dream Car' model, created in the thirties and later brought to a peak in the extravagant and meretricious Hollywood-inspired styling of Harley Earl, now confronted German car manufacturers as they restarted production. It was a major carrier of post-war values, notably conspicuous consumption, so that by the mid-fifties Opel's *Kapitän* with its vestigial tail fins resembled a '52 Chevrolet. Earlier, however, German designers remained rather conservative in their borrowings. In 1948, the year the first Ford *Taunus* left the Cologne factory, the General Motors Opel plant at Rüsselsheim had its first full post-war season producing models that were scaled-down sedans based on pre-war American styles. Gradually the gap between Detroit design and German adaptation shrank. Other cars such as Borgwards made in Bremen would, in the fifties, also aim at the symbolism of wealth and social prestige contained in American limousines. Even the bubble car, whose emergence was an acknowledgement of the comparatively high cost of petrol in Europe, was a miniaturized form of streamlining.

The continuity within streamlining is most evident in the Volkswagen 1200 first produced in 1938, unchanged in 1945 and not withdrawn until 1961. For Hitler, who regarded Henry Ford as the greatest American in history, it was to have been the answer to all those needs Germans shared with Americans. Moreover, as a commodity costing no more than a motor bike and intended by the Nazis (eventually) for numerous classes of ownership, it was regarded as the symbol of the end of class conflict and of the inception of a new united national culture. Similarly, as economic conditions after the war improved and purchasing power slowly returned, possessions such as the Volkswagen, combining American standardization and German technical sophistication, were seen as the harbingers of an affluent middle-class society modelled on the United States. If Borgward and Opel announced that Germany was becoming as modern and progressive as America, Volkswagen in a more recognizably nationalistic fashion epitomized the economic miracle and was saying that Germany was a force to be reckoned with once more. Ironically, it was the British Occupation forces through ingenuity and improvisation who salvaged the Volkswagen factory in 1945 and in the next two years laid the groundwork for its later success.

With 7,000 export orders at the end of 1948 Volkswagen soon became the best-selling imported car in the USA, accepted into a commercial market which demanded both repetition and differentiation. The smooth unruptured continuity of American consumerism and styling was evident at home and abroad. And with the increase in wealth and private goods during the Cold War, the Americanization process in Germany and the rest of Europe began to look like straightforward colonialism.

Chapter nine

The 1950s: Cold War / Hot Sun in Capri

The 1950s were the turning point in the history of Amerika. Those who grew up before the 1950s live today in the mental world of Nazism, concentration camps, economic depression and Communist dreams Stalinized. . . . Kids who grew up in the post-1950s live in a world of supermarkets, color TV commercials, guerrila war, international media psychedelics, rock n'roll and moon walks.
Jerry Rubin, *Do It!*, New York: Simon and Schuster, 1970, pp. 90–1.

Writing in 1924 Virginia Woolf claimed that human nature changed and all human relations shifted 'on or about December 1910'. A similar claim could justifiably be made for post-war Western society. In the case of Germany the date could be pinpointed as precisely as 21 June 1948 when the conversion of the currency transformed German psychology and the commercial environment.[1] That society was ultimately characterized by the visible growth and evident influence of advertising, TV, and other media, by suburbanization and an expanding automobile culture, by visual discourses of fashion and style, and by a pervasive consumer society different in significant ways from its pre-war counterpart.

In studying this phenomenon, Jean Baudrillard has drawn attention to the widespread nature of a surface of signs and also to the way this discourse has transcended the material world of goods. There is, for example, no marketing debate about different breads; rather is the opposition one of *artificiality* (white bread) and *naturalness* (brown bread). 'Everywhere there is substitution, instead and in place of the real, of a "neo-real" produced entirely out of the elements of the codes.'[2] Indeed, consumers actively wish to enter this symbolic universe with its images of an intense 'real life', one which obliges them not only to buy commodities but buy their characteristics as well. The acquisition of symbols involves the transferance of information. Knowledge of both the actual and imagined attributes of commodities increases, thus facilitating the process whereby the need and desire for goods extends to the symbols.

While there is a tendency for attributes to fragment and so produce a fluid, randomized material landscape, circumstances can at times anchor and cement commodities and meanings. The messages carried by consumer goods in the 1950s in Germany were clear and direct: American-style capitalism and the affluent society signified not only happiness but also liberty, freedom, and democracy, abstractions which George V. Allen, director of the US Information Service, described as 'products to sell'. Ludwig Erhard, Minister for Economic Affairs in the Adenauer government, stressed in his 1962 book *Prosperity for All* the logical connection between the freedom of economic enterprise and consumer freedom (in the sense of acting rationally and critically in making consumer choices).

In the second half of the nineteenth century the appearance of department stores in Paris, then in London, New York, and Chicago, along with the development of advertising, were the outward indications of a radical historic shift from production to retail selling and the augmentation of basic needs by created desires. This marked the beginning of modern consumer society.

The early years of the twentieth century in the United States witnessed an acceleration of changes. In the late teens Hollywood and popular literature advocated a new liberated morality and life-style based on leisure and consumerism. The purchase of victrolas, clothes, and cars also brought pleasure and a release from the constraints of Victorian ethics and behaviour. Technology and mass production were playing a major part in putting modern goods within the reach of average Americans. A survey of 100 Ford employees in 1929 revealed that ninety-eight owned new electric irons and almost half owned washing-machines. Already in 1926 a German observer, Julius Hirsch, with a prophetic use of language, had chosen to entitle his study of the United States *Das amerikanische Wirtschaftswunder* (The American Economic Miracle).

Nor did the Depression have a lasting effect upon consumerism.[3] All Roosevelt's important programmes sought to increase the employment and purchasing power of the American public. As one of its major purposes The New York World's Fair (1939–40) promoted the availability of consumer goods and services. To visit the World's Fair was to be immersed in an extraordinarily skilful advertisement for the American way of life and its future extension predicated on technological power and benevolent machinery. During the war, when research promised an aerodynamic, supersonic, electronic world of gadgetry, the utopian discourse became dominant. If not at once, then eventually, according to the prediction of one advertiser, Main Street might look like a comic book concept of the planet Saturn.

With the contrivance of a modest redistribution of wealth, class and regional differences appeared to be dissolving at a time of unprecedented national consolidation: disparate groups and values were fused into a unitary – and optimistic – nationality. Competition from ethnic culture (such as foreign-language newspapers and theatre performances) declined and popular culture, in an increasingly homogenized form, was disseminated through network radio and the mass circulation magazines discussed earlier – *Life*, *Look*, *Reader's Digest*, and the *Saturday Evening Post*. Thus, popular culture, including advertisements, was functioning as propaganda. Consumers were being recruited to say 'yes' to corporate capitalism, but the illusion of freedom of choice was still being promoted. A further illusion, its falsity exposed by the conflict in Vietnam, was that of omnipotence:

> Within the 'World of Tomorrow' advertizing there lay an equally significant assumption that the end of the war would mark the beginning of the American century – the final triumph of American business, American technology, American political leadership, American values.[4]

While the mass media were sanctioning views to which widespread consent had already been given, signs of social stress were becoming apparent. Somehow the brave new world of technology had to assimilate the values of the past, of the Capraesque small town pastoral with its corner drugstore, white picket fences, Main Street marching bands, pie-baking rituals, and genial, contented families. The threats posed by modernity are registered with different degrees of intensity in such films as *It's a Wonderful Life* and *The Best Years of Our Lives* (both 1946).

The emergence of an affluent society in the decades after the Second World War still looked like the unproblematic fulfilment of recent prophecies. In the USA a 'democratic' attitude towards commodities accepted that the greatest possible number of people should enjoy their possession. This approach to marketing, which included lower-income groups, was obviously not present in Europe in 1945 but was available in subsequent decades.

A feature article in *Time* magazine (1 November 1948) demonstrated how swiftly the assumption of an economy and social environment comparable to that of the United States took place in Germany after the currency reform earlier in the year. German industry was starting to operate at full blast. By the spring of 1948 it had achieved 57 per cent of its 1936 level, reaching the pre-war level by the end of 1949. Exports doubled in volume between 1948 and 1949 and were worth DM8,000 million in 1950. Large new neon signs sprang up; Frankfurt's *Bahnhofplatz* came to resemble a corner of New York's Times Square. The reduction of tax on unearned income favoured the rich, who could be seen in their chauffeur-driven cars (Taunuses or imported Chevrolets), perhaps on their way to one of those extravagant luncheons that started in American style with a round of martinis. In Munich at any rate these were not black marketeers or *nouveaux riches* spivs, but wealthy industrialists, aristocrats in 'folk-suits', gentlemen farmers, bureaucrats, and similar officials. Smart cafés and night-clubs were among the tourist attractions beginning to proliferate in the cities. The economic miracle also took place just as dramatically in the countryside where the second homes of the bourgeoisie would become a common sight.[5]

Later, skyscrapers of glass, steel, and plastic arose out of the ruins echoing American attributes of strength, size, and efficiency. The Berlin Hilton, costing $6·5 million and designed by American architects Pereira and Luckman, epitomized the 'society of the spectacle' in the sense of capital accumulated to the degree that it becomes a superficial but all-embracing, glamorous image. At the Hollywood-style opening in 1958, bell-hops with pocket radios attended to the needs of celebrities specially flown in from New York. An earlier example of resurgent national power was the completion in the winter of 1951–2 of Germany's first post-war ocean liner built with American money. Nationalism was also to the fore in the revival of the Wagner cult with Bayreuth now the highspot of the social season, staging not only opera but vulgar displays of vast wealth. As Adorno observed, in *In Search of Wagner*, 1981, (original German version 1952), the homogenization of music, word, and image in Wagner's operas anticipated features of the Hollywood film. More relevant to the fifties is his observation that the operas are commodities in which the tableaux resemble goods on display. While presenting a version of the banal world of the German Empire, they also conjured up a mythic, pre-modern past so that, like the *Heimatfilme*, the *Gesamtkunstwerk* permitted an escape from capitalist fragmentation and alienation.

In increasing numbers Germans travelled to the USA where, it was said, they were visiting their own liberal capitalist future. Like immigrants in their own country they would become absorbed into a global mass culture. A mark of the more receptive climate in the United States was the Goethe Centennial (June 1949), the brainchild of Robert Hutchins, president of the University of Chicago, and sponsored in Aspen, Colorado by its most powerful inhabitant Walter Paepcke, president of the Container Corporation of America. The evocation of the Goethe spirit was looked upon as a remedy for the post-war crisis of Western culture. A distinguished list of the sort of cultural commentators to be found in *Der Monat* was engaged as speakers: Stephen Spender, Ortega y Gasset, Thornton Wilder, and Albert Schweitzer. The previous summer had witnessed the start of the Berlin blockade, so that the language of the publicity surrounding the event had an extra political dimension. East Germany acknowledged this by organizing its own celebration of Goethe as an exponent of world Communism.

The centennial turned out to be not only a celebration of liberal humanism but also a demonstration of the pervasive irresistible nature of mass culture and advertising. A campaign mounted by the Chicago public relations firm Mitchell McKeown covered all forms of media communication and included the promotion in shops and women's magazines of 'Philosophic Fashions'. . . .

Publicity photos included a 'grizzled miner' buying his tickets with silver dollars at the Goethe Office. Visitors from most American states were lured to Aspen; unfortunately, some betrayed their ignorance by asking where they could actually meet Mr 'Goity' or 'Goweth'.

Meanwhile, in Goethe's native land the urban conglomerations along the Rhine and parallel to the Elbe were turning part of West Germany into a single megalopolis resembling the east coast of America. '*Tausendgut – Güldenfatt – Rosenschleck* (thousands of goods – golden fat – rosy candy)' was the poet Peter Rühmkorf's pithy description of the ethos of the new republic.[6] Brecht's *Deutschland, bleiche Mutter* (Germany, pale mother) was now in Ruhmkorf's eyes *Käufliche Mutter* (Mother for sale). The cultural imperialism of the United States was matched by the eagerness of Germans – and other Europeans – to have American products and to adopt American life-styles. However, many were less eager to undergo the consequences of becoming America's main European ally: rearmament and military service.

During those initial years of prosperity, 30–40 per cent of commodities were being bought by only 10 per cent of the population and most Germans were limited to the pleasures of window-shopping. For them this was truly (in Ursula Wassermann's report on Hamburg's prosperity in 1952) '*Schlaraffenland*–the never never land of which hungry stomachs dream at night'.[7] Outward appearances to the contrary, consumption was damped down in favour of production, priority was given to the export trade, and profits were put back into industry. The policy was a long-term one with the result that, between 1950 and 1960, real personal income in the *Bundesrepublik* rose faster and farther than anywhere in the world. If affluence was yet to spread throughout German society the range available in 1950 (as a consequence of hoarding savings and, illegally, stocks of goods) was already quite remarkable: 'Every consumer good can be purchased from modern and antique furniture to airplane tickets, from barometers to leather goods, from fur coats to French perfume, from radios and mechanical household equipment to books and pictures.'[8] Most middle-class houses in the fifties acquired washing-machines, food blenders, and refrigerators, and by the end of the sixties Erhard's encouragement of hire purchase meant that manual workers were able to buy television sets and to take holidays abroad.

The 'freedom' and 'equality' implied by the economic miracle were but illusions in the fifties, when luxuries remained for many just a vision, part of a promise that bourgeois society would develop into a society of plenitude for all, a democracy of abundance which socialism had been unable to deliver. It would not be a society interested in, say, attractive low-cost public housing and, as in the USA, the term 'proletarian' became regarded as offensive. (As Americans became more successful, few wanted to recall the poverty of the Depression years.) Consumer goods from the United States (Coca-Cola, jeans, American-styled cars, and so on), whether actually possessed or appropriated visually through styles and fashions, symbolized modern American society and its affluence. This allowed Germans to participate in an individualized and loose bourgeois milieu, very different from the traditional German system, which, with its emphasis on authority, was still ideologically dominant in certain areas of public life.

The idea of free enterprise and *Spiessbürgertum* (bourgeois conformism) was combined with pro-Americanism and anti-Communism. A spate of war films at this time including American-produced examples reflected the cultural and political importance of the fierce rearmament debate taking place. Kautner's 1956 film version of *The Captain of Köpenick* even subtly reversed the anti-militarism of Carl Zuckmayer's 1931 play. Suffused with sexism and a sentimental nationalism centred on Berlin and its culture (a city of increased symbolic significance to West Germans since the blockade), the film moves its outsider protagonist towards reconciliation with the status quo. Anti-militarist figures are mocked and the existence of a military class accepted despite its reprehensible exclusiveness. This elitism will be remedied in the contemporary world by the 'democracy' and civic education requirement of the *Bundeswehr* founded in the same year.

Nationalism and sentimentality were also present in a resurgence of 'Heimat' films, beginning in 1950 with a remake of *Black Forest Maiden* (1933). Viewed from a broad historical perspective their rural traditional values and picture-postcard cultural *kitsch* can be interpreted as the fantasy projections of a shattered nation under occupation and thus powerful negative images of the reconstructing, outwardly progressive Federal

Republic. Americanization helped to determine contemporary film genres with 'holiday' and road movies propagating the values of mobility and consumerism for a population increasingly able to take holidays abroad in romantic resorts epitomized by sunny Capri. (Hawaii performed a similar function for the newly affluent Japanese.) In addition films catering to a growing youth culture (such as *Peter and Conny machen Musik*) imitated American models such as rock 'n' roll movies, while Horst Buchholz in *Die Halbstarken* (The Hooligans) earned the description: a synthetic copy of Marlon Brando and James Dean. Heinz Abosch was moved to write at the end of the decade:

> If West Germany is beyond question the most American country outside America, it is the young Germans who are most completely americanized. Meeting them in the evening, in the American-made pin-table saloons, or skylarking on their noisy motor-bikes, you come across so many James Deans, Marlon Brandos and Marilyn Monroes that you scarcely know which country you are in![9]

Like traditional Hollywood, German cinema of the fifties was not interested in the real lives of office workers, students, or farm labourers. Instead, the values of power, authority, and obedience were supported with the historical image of a wise, benevolent ruler or leader frequently produced on screen: a clear reference to the 'enlightened' regime of Konrad Adenauer. The speeches of the first post-war Chancellor were drawn upon for the background of fifties Germany in Rainer Werner Fassbinder's *The Marriage of Maria Braun* (1979). In that film and its successors, inspired by the ambivalent Hollywood melodramas of Douglas Sirk, Fassbinder's intention was to analyse critically the values (especially the sentimental idealism) of Germany in the decades following 'Year Zero'. 'The old order renewed itself with financial aid and military support for its new American partners before continuing on in the old familiar way.'[10]

The world of painting was also the site of cultural hegemony and contradiction as well as further evidence of commodification. The rapid homogenization of ideology and culture which took place in the Federal Republic also resulted in the demonizing of theories and perspectives from behind the Iron Curtain. Stylistically, abstraction and the non-representational were all the rage.

After 1953 Realism was considered a culturally backward concept. It was left to the Eastern Bloc, while West Germany also in a cultural sense joined the other victorious powers . . . Art, too, had been enlisted into the service of the Cold War.[11]

The elevation of objectivity and autonomy as artistic criteria was, in the context of international power relations, a contradiction and a deception. Nevertheless, the whole abstract expressionist movement in Europe unequivocally endorsed (and was an extension of) American strength, vigour, wealth, and beliefs. A national American art had with determination become international and to claim in Germany in the mid-fifties that the abstract movement had a global character was to connote America's global mission and the Coca-Colonization of culture in Europe. American art and culture were now engaged in the same work as American foreign policy, preserving and seeking to demonstrate democratic liberty and freedom of expression.

All this was a long way from the individual concerns of the major American abstract expressionists. Barnett Newman and Hans Hofmann both stressed the centrality of subject matter, while the sculptor David Smith insisted that there was no such thing as art that was 'truly abstract' (original emphasis). Their concern with the subject (the 1978 Abstract Expressionist Exhibition at the National Gallery of Art in Washington was entitled 'The Subjects of the Artist') was accompanied by the urge to maintain artistic integrity, to move away from the surrealism they had once found liberating but whose smooth clean surfaces had become in the forties the property of advertisers.

Abstract expressionism was to suffer the same fate. Modern industry and commerce, seeking to show their sophistication and to pre-empt any charge of philistine materialism, publicly gave support and patronage to abstract art, awarding prizes, publishing the periodical *Jahresring* (Annual Tree-ring), and flooding museums with gifts. In the United States, prompted by magazines such as *Life* and *Harper's Bazaar*, upper middle-class Americans began in the mid-forties to embellish their homes with modern paintings, which were also lucrative investments. Now in the following decade ambitious executives and bureaucrats in Germany also sought to decorate their apartments and houses with contemporary artworks and non-representational motifs, some-times in incongruous juxtaposition with older national German styles in art and fittings:

> No wealthy upstart's home is considered complete without a fake baroque angel alongside the built-in bar, . . . Next to a dining-room furnished in Old German farm-house style, you are sure to find a few pieces of ultra modern design.[12]

In contrast there was a further realm of cultural activity in West Germany: the conglomeration of romance, comic strips, *Heimat-filme*, and soft pornography, epitomized by the sensational Ameri-canized tabloid *Bild-Zeitung* – crude, schmaltzy, philistine, prurient, and fiercely anti-left. Intellectuals recoiled from this strident form of populism: the *nouveaux riches*, by absorbing and digesting contemporary art, made common cause with them, as Jost Hermand explains in a brilliant article.[13] Ironically, however, by incorporating within consumer society the latest fashions of modernist painting and design, the newly affluent were turning works of art into desirable retail goods, packaged fragments of that same Americanized mass culture.

The conformism outlined above was symbolized in the United States by suburban tract housing or dormitory communities for white-collar workers which became an obsession for some journa-lists, academics, and novelists. Best-selling novels such as Sloan Wilson's *The Man in the Gray Flannel Suit* (1955) offered a corporate, middle-class pattern of success in which the boredom and reduced possibilities of a career, not as a high-flying executive but as a cog-like organization man, are justified on the grounds that 'an island of order in a sea of chaos' is thereby made attainable. That island of order is the small, private world of family life.

For women in American popular novels, success remained confined within the roles of mother and wife, their rewards being the material ones of a sumptuously furnished middle-class home. In Germany during the war Nazi propaganda emphasized the necessity of functioning as wife and mother: unlike their Ameri-can counterparts German bourgeois women responded feebly to exhortations urging them to take up war work in the factories. After 1945, though, women, often widowed or abandoned, sought to be integrated into the labour force in order to support themselves and their families. In Berlin 60,000 *Trümmerfrauen* (Rubble-women) spent years clearing thousands of tons of debris from the city's streets and squares for a wage insufficient to buy a loaf of bread a week on the black market. As manual labourers, however, they were allowed extra food rations.

As buildings of glass and chrome appeared to replace the rubble in the period of the economic miracle, German women became attracted by the idea of America and a leisure society: newspapers and magazines bulged with pages of advertisements for glamorous clothes and exotic food. As early as 1946 Margaret Bourke-White, selecting photographic subjects in Germany, had noted that the bodies of sunbathing – and fraternizing – *Fräuleins* had 'a sleek American look'. In the fifties, however, others were more impressed by the numbers of women in American public life and by the greater control over their lives accorded to married women. This had been acknowledged by a *March of Time* newsreel in 1948 which presented women judges, educators, and journalists, though it also stressed the business/consumption link by focusing upon careers in fashion.

The concept of the 'good housemother' (*Kinder, Küche, Kirche*) nevertheless survived, and was supported in such books as Hilde Thurnwald's *Gegenwartsprobleme Berliner Familien*, which in 1948 described the housewife in Victorian terms as guardian of the house and loving, nurturing, healing centre of the family. Similar ideas were promulgated in conservative 'marriage' films of the fifties which failed to address the real problems of gender and relationships between the sexes. At about the same time the participation of women in the reconstruction of Germany came to an end. As Fassbinder would show in *The Marriage of Maria Braun*, scarcely had the women cleared the rubble than the men returned to power.

In 1949 the West German Constitution granted women equality with men before the law, although as Erica Carter has pointed out women's citizenship came to be defined through consumption in a social market economy. Ms Carter has spotlighted female adolescent consumption as a separate and special area:

The word teenager first entered the German language in the 1950s, imported like chewing gum and Coca-Cola from the

USA and vibrant with connotations of crazy styles, zany humour, rock 'n' roll parties, Elvis, James Dean, loud music and soft park-bench romance.[14]

Only the USA among industrial nations could provide teenagers with satisfying images of modernity and subcultural style that also functioned as stimuli to demand. Such teenagers preferred American off-the-peg clothes, including jeans, a uniform reminiscent of GI dungarees. They read media and fashion weeklies such as *Bravo*, which in the late fifties ran a series of advertisements for seamless stockings (a commodity apparently already owned by *Bravo* female readers). The magazine also carried reports of Mamoulian's remake of the movie *Ninotchka* entitled *Silk Stockings*, which the *Bravo* article oversimplified as the opposition between Moscow/politics and USA/democracy/silk stockings. Ignoring the ambiguities of the film established by dance, energy, and spontaneity, *Bravo* in its review stressed femininity, defined by the consumption of fashion items, and American triumph in the East–West conflict.

Just as important for a consideration of Americanization is the relationship between certain images mentioned by Ms Carter. These are the American GI offering black market nylons at the end of the war and secondly, poster graphics of the fifties depicting stockinged female legs as symbolic of a revived, flourishing European economy. Superimposition exposes such meanings as the black market (the Berlin-to-Osnabrück train was known as the Silk Stocking Express), the Marshall Plan, consumer democracy, and the American way of life.

The arrival of the word 'teenager' in Germany referred to above implies two of many criticisms levelled at the outward forms of the economic miracle: the defilement of the German language and, with the emergence of a new Americanized generation, a break with inherited cultural values and the cherished sense of community or *Gemeinschaft*. Such values were, it was thought, being supplanted by a second-hand lifestyle, one which in a 1957 Dutch newspaper report was described as untidy and brutal:

> The streets are wide, lined with glass buildings, gleaming with metal, everywhere department stores. . . . All this is no longer German, it is American. The shop windows, glowing

and shining, give an impression of excess . . . the new streets appear crude and bombastic.[15]

Crude or not, Americanization was one aspect of the amnesiac impulse in the post-war period, the wish to regard the Third Reich as a bad dream. For the man or woman in the street serious issues apart from West Germany's economic resurgence were boring or disturbing. Consumer democracy, a self-referential world that could replace the historical world of experience, was one means of blotting out the years of the Nazi regime. It was also daily evidence of the relationship with another state – the USA – where a reluctant engagement with history had long been a feature of national consciousness.

Some observers, especially intellectuals and writers, made the traumatic discovery that the past had not been sufficiently demolished, that war criminals were now working in the police force and that former Nazis, men who had worked for and shared the politics of Krupp and Thyssen, had been brought in along with members of those notorious families to help in the rebuilding of German industry. With old Nazis reinstated and giving jobs to party cronies, a microcosm of Hitler's state was gradually being created within West Germany's bureaucracy, judiciary, and diplomatic service. Even at the end of the war ex-Nazis awaiting interrogation in the Western zones had enjoyed better rations than most Germans.

Walter Abish's remarkable novel *How German Is It* (1980) is more concerned with quests and, as the title hints, questions than with standard responses to modern German history and the *Wirtschaftswunder*. Abish is interested not merely in West Germany but also in 'Germany', an imaginary invented place: even so the bland suburbs of Brumholdstein where the newly affluent reside have been built on the site of the Nazi concentration camp, Durst. Born in Vienna, Abish became an American citizen in 1960 but *How German Is It* is less involved with cultural Americanization than certain German novels of the fifties which anatomized the economic miracle from the perspective of both the right and the left. Gerd Gaiser's *Schlussball* (1958), published in Britain as *The Last Dance of the Season*, is set in the small country town of Neu-Spuhl shortly after the currency reform. The townsfolk are preoccupied with money, possessions, and local industry. Americanization is to blame and Gaiser contrasts the noble struggles of wartime survivors in 1945 and after with the greed, spiritual emptiness, and conformity of 'mass-produced *homo spulicus*'. The author's indignation is provoked not only by suburbanization but also by the pollution and defoliation of nature, the spread of foul red dust from Neu-Spuhl's factory. The town's expansion is inexorable and the results horrific: 'the gigantic dumps of bottles and tins under which the last murmur of brooks were being suffocated; the refuse and the discoloured scum in the stinking gutters' (pp. 34–5).

Two years later Martin Walser in *Halbzeit* (Half-time) seized on a number of interlinked targets. At the end of the war the Catholic Church and the Communists shared in the hope of a new, more just society. Here, in contrast, the Church, represented by Father Burgstaller, reveres President Eisenhower as the leader of the Christian camp and reviles Communism as the anti-Christ. The strength and penetration of an ideology comprising bourgeois consumerism and anti-Communism is a major constituent of the novel's meaning. The wealthy Frantzke family business is run on American lines and Walser is particularly responsive to the Americanized jargon of German advertising men (*Accountexekutive, Lay-Outer, das Research, die Publicity, public relations, Campaign, Food-Konzern*) as well as to the snobbish use of Anglo-American terms generally in affluent West German business and social circles. Some years earlier special dictionaries had started to appear catering for the varied requirements of industry, business, and management. A. Heidelberger's *Wörterbuch der amerikanischen Verwaltungssprache* (administrative language) in 1948 provided an extensive list of abbreviations customary in US offices, while Richard Webster's *Dictionary of Marketing Terms* in 1952 listed (with translations) the current jargon in the fields of market research, advertising, and public relations.

Other phrases arising from Walser's satire of the marketing milieu are 'Manipulation des Image' and 'Human Engineering'. Consciousness control or propaganda which endeavours to replace understanding with an indoctrinated faith is now, through the American connection, regarded as respectable, though Walser makes the ironic point that a number of American writers (notably Vance Packard) have exposed 'the hidden persuaders'. In *Halbzeit* this *method* of selling resembles that used by the Third Reich. Goebbels is admired by Dr Fuchs who perceives the one-time

Reichsminister as the precursor of modern advertising strategy. With the purpose of political conditioning removed, the strategy is quite acceptable in a consumer-oriented society.

Walser's demonstration of continuity is a reminder that the admiration of all things American in the 1950s should not be considered or interpreted in an historical vacuum. What was sometimes referred to as 'daily colonialism' had its roots in both the pre-war period and the era of re-education. For Walter Laqueur to argue that 'no one had ever been forced to drink Coca Cola rather than lemonade or wine, eat a hamburger rather than a German beef steak or Sauerbraten' is to ignore wilfully the history and nature of American influence. Nor does the persuasive statement that few would be alive on the planet if Germany had emulated the military strength of the United States justify describing a new McDonald's in 1982 as an 'island of hospitality'.[16]

Attitudes towards post-war German consumer society will change as generations succeed one another. Quitt, a businessman–poet in Peter Handke's play *They Are Dying Out* (1975), looks back on the years of the economic miracle with a nostalgia that survives the dramatist's irony:

> Suddenly I saw an old poster hoarding. In those days I used to read everything on it. Now the hoarding was nearly empty, only one poster left, an ad for a powdered milk that's long off the market. (*He raises his arms.*) While I drove slowly past, the posters for all the bygone chocolates, tooth pastes and elections passed before my mind's eye, and in this gentle moment of recollection, I was overcome by a profound sense of history.[17]

The feeling expressed here can also be located in the paintings of Roy Lichtenstein and the plays of Sam Shepard. As society discards old products in a hectic race to 'make it new', the outmoded consumer object attains a special status. In its nostalgic setting it becomes America's historical ruin and has given rise to an eclectic post-modernist fascination with cultural signs.

In the 1960s, long before Handke's play, young Germans still recalled the goodwill of Americans in the form of CARE packages, for example. Nevertheless, American soldiers were often treated with contempt by students and the intellectual classes; the cry went out for cultural decolonization. (Today cultural antipathy and political condemnation go hand in hand.) These reactions conveniently side-stepped the genuine material improvements to the lives of many people in West Germany. In addition, to rail against materialism, popular entertainment and *kitsch* in a world whose contemporary history is riddled with instances of barbarism might suggest to many a distorted sense of priorities. Yet it must be added that while the public aspires to a condition of prosperity, its members also deserve community and a true democracy. Addressing an SPD rally in Hamburg in September 1977, the Swiss playwright Max Frisch expressed a hope for 'greater democracy'. 'That goal' he asserted, 'would be far superior to those of selfish consumerism.'

It is not unnatural to recoil from the manipulations of advertisers or to feel oppressed by what Jackson Lears has called 'the masked ball of market society'. In the afterword to *Out of the Shelter*, his novel set in the American zone after the war, David Lodge describes the hedonistic world of American consumerism as 'a life of possessions, of personal transportation, labour-saving devices, smart cheap clothing, mass tourism, technologically-based leisure and entertainment.'[18] He then proceeds to ask whether this constitutes freedom or enslavement. Prosperity in itself does not necessarily lead to a denial of ethics, the crushing of conscience, and the homogenization of the arts. It may however create a culture of narcissism whose citizens are spectators without communal loyalties and a society of rising crime and suicide rates, one that is indifferent, greedy, and lacking in moral concern. One problem now facing consumer societies, all deeply inscribed by Americanization, is the political and social means by which such a fate is averted, a fate which continues to threaten the cities of the USA itself:

Flashes forward

In Wim Wenders' movie *Summer in the City* (1970) an image of part of an Amoco petrol station reads: AMOC.

The 750th anniversary of Berlin (30 May 1987).
A few miles south-east of the Kurfürstendamm, where the appearance of smart cafés and expensive retail stores announced the beginning of a consumer paradise in the 1950s, lies the district of

Kreuzberg (known as 'Little Istanbul'). A burnt-out supermarket, wrecked cars, and anarchist graffiti show a frustration about deprivation and poverty being expressed in looting and violence.

Notes

Preface

1. S. Frederick Starr, in his excellent book on jazz in Russia, *Red and Hot; The Fate of Jazz in the Soviet Union* (Oxford University Press, New York, 1983) grants the diversity and richness of American popular culture, but considers jazz the most influential art form in its effects upon other states and peoples.

Chapter one: Cultural Interactions and Perceptions in the American Zone

1. The American zone consisted of Greater Hesse, Bavaria, and Baden-Württemberg.
2. Edwin Hartrich, *The Fourth and Richest Reich*, New York: Collier-Macmillan, 1980, p. 53.
3. John A. Gimbel, *A German Community under American Occupation: Marburg 1945–52*, Stanford: Stanford University Press, 1961, esp. p. 202.
4. Josef Joffe, 'The greening of Germany', *The New Republic* 14 (February 1983): 18.
5. Melvin Lasky, 'Berlin Letter', *Partisan Review* XV, 1 (January 1948): 60.
6. Gimbel, *A German Community*, p. 17: 'Marburgers . . . were impressed by the apparently endless columns of tanks, trucks, half-trucks, jeeps and other vehicles of the American Army that passed through Marburg's narrow streets.' Also Hartrich, *The Fourth and Richest Reich*, pp. 41– 2: 'The main floor of the Barter Mart [in Frankfurt] resembled a vast general store, a sort of supermarket crossed with an antique shop . . . Everything from an etching by Albrecht Durer to a can of Crisco [was on sale].'
7. In 1948, the dump in Berlin where the American Army HQ disposed of its refuse was continuously populated by men, women, and children searching for cigarettes, orange, and grapefruit peel

(for soup) and toothpaste. Shortages of food, coal, and clothing were, of course, exacerbated by the activities of racketeers.

8. See Jan Dawson, *Wim Wenders*, Toronto: Toronto Film Festival, 1976.
9. Barbara Mettler, *Demokratisierung und Kalter Krieg: zur amerikanischen Informations- und Rundfunkpolitik in West Deutschland 1945–1949*, Berlin: Spiess, 1975, p. 104.
10. Hans Habe, *Our Love Affair with Germany*, New York: Putnam, 1953, p. 19.
11. *Radio Illustrierte Bremen*, 14 (1948): 3.
12. Richard J. Barnet, *Allies: America–Europe–Japan Since the War*, New York: Simon and Schuster, 1983, pp. 38, 50.
13. Wolfgang Kreuter and Joachim Oltmann, '*Coca-Cola statt Apfelmost: Kalter Krieg und Amerikanisierung westdeutscher Lebenweise*', Englisch-Amerikanische Studien, Marz 1/84, p. 24.
14. See Charles Higham, *Trading With the Enemy: An Exposé of the Nazi–American Money Plot, 1933–1949*, London: Hale, 1983.
15. Franz L. Neumann, 'Re-educating the Germans: the dilemma of reconstruction', *Commentary*, June 1947, p. 525.
16. Nicholas Pronay and Keith Wilson (eds), *The Political Re-Education of Germany and her Allies after World War II*, London/Sydney: Croom Helm, 1985, 'Introduction', p. 11.
17. Later the adoption of Western boots, jeans, and windcheaters modelled on US Air Force flight jackets earned the label 'Primitive Americanism'.
18. Richard J. Grunberger, *A Social History of the Third Reich*, London: Weidenfeld, 1971, p. 33.
19. Kreuter and Oltmann, '*Coca-Cola statt Apfelmost*', p. 28.
20. Anna J. and Richard L. Merritt (eds), *Public Opinion in Occupied Germany: The OMGUS Surveys, 1945–1949*, Urbana: University of Illinois Press, 1970, p. 184.
21. Jean-François Lyotard, *Instructions paiennes*, Paris: Galilee, 1977, p. 39.
22. Branches of McDonalds have provided sites for anti-American demonstrations. For West German teenagers, however, immersed in an urban youth culture of styles, music, and consumerism, they have provided late afternoon week-end way-stations.

Chapter two: Re-education: 'Your Job in Germany'

1. Quoted in James F. Tent, *Mission on the Rhine; Re-education and Denazification in American-Occupied Germany*, Chicago: University of Chicago Press, 1983, p. 299.
2. 'Should we trade teachers with Germany?', *Saturday Evening Post*, 17 April 1948, p. 142.
3. Sigmund Skard, *American Studies in Europe: Their History and Present Organization*, Philadelphia: University of Pennsylvania Press, 1958, vol. 1, p. 326.

4. Karl-Ernst Bungenstab, 'Entstehung, Bedeutungs- und Funktionswandel der Amerika-Häuser. Ein Beitrag zur Geschichte der amerikanischen Auslandsinformation nach dem 2. Weltkrieg', *Jahrbuch fur Amerikastudien* band 16 (1971): 194–5.

5. ibid., p. 197.

6. Henry P. Pilgert, *The History of the Development of Information Services through Information Centers and 'Documentary Films*, Historical Division Office of the Exec. Secretary, Office of the US High Commissioner for Germany, 1951, p. 39.

7. See Michael Hoenisch, 'Film as an instrument of the U.S. Re-education Program in Germany after 1945 and the example of "Todesmühlen" ', *Englisch–Amerikanische Studien* 4 (1–2) (1982): 201. I am indebted to Dr Hoenisch's article for many details. Also valuable is Stuart Schulbert, 'Of All People', *Hollywood Quarterly* 4 (1949–50): 206–8.

8. Edward N. Petersen, *Retreat to Victory: The American Occupation of Germany*, Detroit: Wayne State University Press, 1978, p. 34.

Chapter three: Film: The Affair of Billy Wilder's *A Foreign Affair*

1. Figures from Thomas Guback, 'Shaping the film business in postwar Germany: the role of the US film industry and the US state', in Paul Kerr (ed.) *The Hollywood Film Industry* London and New York: Routledge and Kegan Paul, 1986, pp. 245–7.

2. Quoted in Roger Manvell, *Films and the Second World War*, London: Dent, 1974, p. 203.

3. Billy Wilder, 'Propaganda Through Entertainment', US Forces European Theater, Information Control Division, memo to Davidson Taylor, 16 August 1945. A German version, 'Propaganda durch Unterhaltung' is in Brewster S. Chamberlin, *Kultur auf Trümmern: Berliner Berichte der Amerikanischen Information Control Section*, Juli–Dezember, 1945 (Stuttgart, 1979), pp. 99–103. Dr Chamberlin's generous assistance, particularly in the provision of materials and information, has been crucial in the preparation of this chapter. Assistance has also been kindly provided by Kenneth Short and David Culbert.

4. I am grateful to the Motion Picture Broadcasting and Recorded Sound Division of the Library of Congress for enabling me to view their copy of *A Foreign Affair*.

5. OWI Regional Directive, Overseas Branch, 5 February 1945; RG 208 Box 808, OWI Records, WNRC. For the Government Manual (1942) see K.R.M. Short, 'Washington's Information Manual for Hollywood, 1942', *Historical Journal of Film, Radio and Television* 3(2) (1983): 171–80.

6. 'It was less interested in direct large scale American re-education efforts than in Germany's restauration by the old "enlightened"

Weimar elite.' Karl Heinz Putz, 'Business or propaganda? American films and Germany, 1942–1946', *Englische-Amerikanische Studien* 2–3, September (1983): 405.

7. ibid., p. 412. See also pp. 406–7 for an account of changing OMGUS attitudes and for the US film industry's penetration of the German market between 1948 and 1952.

8. Albert Norman, *Our German Policy: Propaganda and Culture*, New York: Vantage Press, 1951, p. 64.

9. This phrase from Wilder's memorandum becomes, in modified form, part of Captain Pringle's dialogue in an important scene with Miss Frost:

> You expect him [the GI in Germany] to be an ambassador, a salesman of goodwill. You want him to stand there on the blackened rubble of what used to be the corner of what used to be a street with an open sample case of assorted freedoms waving the flag and giving out with the Bill of Rights. Well that's not the way it works.

10. I have been unable to locate the precise details from the Congressional Record.

11. Herbert Luft, 'A matter of decadence', *Quarterly of Film, Radio and TV* VII (1952–3): 65.

12. Stuart Schulberg, 'A communication: a letter about Billy Wilder', *Quarterly of Film, Radio and TV* VII (1952–3): 435.

13. Quoted in Tom Wood, *The Bright Side of Billy Wilder, Primarily*, New York: Doubleday, 1970, p. 96.

14. See, for example, David Culbert, 'American film policy in the re-education of Germany after 1945', in Nicholas Pronay and Keith Wilson (eds.) *The Political Re-education of Germany and Her Allies After World War II*, London and Sydney: Croom Helm, 1985, pp. 173–95.

15. Michael Hoenisch, 'Film as an instrument of the U.S. Re-education Program in Germany after 1945 and the example of "*Todesmühlen*" ', *Englisch–Amerikanische Studien* 4 (1–2) (1982): pp. 196–210, especially p. 202.

Chapter four: Art and Architecture: From Wasteland to Late Modernism

1. Wieland Schmied, 'Points of departure and transformations in German art 1905–1985', in Christos M. Joannides, Norman Rosenthal and Wieland Schmied (eds) *German Art in the Twentieth Century, Painting and Sculpture 1905–1985*, London: Royal Academy of Arts, 1985, p. 59.

2. See Siegfried Gohr, 'Art in the post-war period', in Joannides, Rosenthal and Schmied (eds), *German Art in the Twentieth Century*, p. 467.

3. Schmied, 'Points of departure and transformations in German art 1905–1985', p. 56. East Germans made similar claims for international recognition.

4. Hubert Hoffmann, 'New German architecture', in Charles E. McClelland and Steven P. Scher (eds) *Postwar German Culture: an Anthology*, New York: Dutton, 1974, p. 408.
5. Hoffmann, 'New German architecture', p. 415.
6. Peter Blake, 'German architecture and American', *Architectural Forum* 107 (August 1957): 133.

Chapter five: Fiction and Drama: That's Entertainment!

1. John R. Frey, 'Postwar German reactions to American literature', *Journal of English and Germanic Philology* LIV (1955): 185.
2. Malcolm Cowley, 'Hemingway at midnight', *The New Republic* CXI (14 August 1944): 190–5, German translation in *Umschau* II, 1947, pp. 542–50.
3. James Jones, *From Here to Eternity*, New York: Collins, 1979, p. 275.
4. Mary Gaither and Horst Frenz, 'German criticism of American drama', *American Quarterly* VII (2) (Summer 1955): 116.
5. John van Druten, *The Voice of the Turtle*, in John Gassner (ed.) *Best Plays of the Modern American Theatre*, Second Series, New York: Crown, 1947, p. 243.
6. Paul Fussell, Jr, 'Thornton Wilder and the German psyche', *The Nation*, 3 May 1958, p. 394.
7. 'Historical Report of Operations of the OMG, Berlin District', 1 July 1945 – 30 June 1946, vol. VIII, Information Control.
8. Thornton Wilder, *Our Town and Other Plays*, Harmondsworth: Penguin, 1962, Preface, p. 13.
9. Robert Ardrey, *Plays of Three Decades*, London: Collins, 1968, pp. 86, 78.

Chapter six: Magazines: Fantasy Unlimited

1. John Lukacs, *1945: Year Zero*, New York: Doubleday, Garden City, 1978, pp. 211–12.
2. Heinz Abosch, *The Menace of the Miracle: Germany from Hitler to Adenauer*, London: Colet's, 1962, p. 107.
3. Robert T. Elson, *The World of Time Inc.: the Intimate History of a Publishing Enterprise, vol. 2, 1947–1960*, New York: Athaneum Press, 1973, p. 189.
4. Frank W. Fox, *Madison Avenue Goes to War: The Strange Military Career of Advertising 1941–45*, Provo, Utah: Brigham Young University Press, 1975, p. 58.
5. *Time* carried advertisements for agents who would ship food (ranging from powdered eggs and chocolate to olive oil, peaches, and salmon) and cigarettes (to United States citizens only) across to Europe. For those American troops serving in Germany, a more luxurious offer was available: British cars, to be paid for in dollars, would be shipped from London to Frankfurt after the completion of each sale.

6. Joseph Goulden, *The Best Years*, New York: Athaneum Press, 1976, p. 6.
7. *Life*, 6 June 1949, p. 12.
8. Similarly, in Botho Strauss's 1978 play *Gross und Klein*, the characters, citizens of the now prosperous Federal Republic, are bemused by the fact that 'instead of war we have this'.
9. Henry P. Pilgert, *Press, Radio and Film in West Germany*, Historical Division, Office of the Executive Secretary, Office of US High Commission for Germany, 1953, p. 15.
10. Hans Magnus Enzensberger, 'Die Sprache des Spiegel', *Der Spiegel*, 6 März 1957, p. 49.

Chapter seven: Jazz: The Sound of Democracy

1. Mike Zwerin, *La Tristesse de Saint Louis: Swing under the Nazis* (Quartet, London, 1985), p. 180.
2. Fred Ritzel, 'Populäre Musik in Deutschland und die Stunde Null', transcript of a conference lecture, Braunschweig, October 1985, p. 5.
3. Hans Peter Bleuel, *Das saubere Reich* (Lubbe, Bergisch Gladbach, 1979), p. 313. See also Martin Chalmers, 'Swingtime for Hitler', *New Musical Express*, 8 September 1986, pp. 20–1. The BBC used this title for a short programme about 'Charlie and his Orchestra' (Radio 4, 16 August 1987).
4. Quoted in Detlev J.K. Peukert, *Inside Nazi Germany: Conformity, Opposition and Racism in Everyday Life* (Batsford, London, 1987), p. 201.
5. Ritzel, 'Populäre Musik . . . ', p. 6.
6. Andi Brauer, 'Schaukeln und Walzen' (Rock'n'Roll) in Eckhard Stepmann (ed.), *Bikini: die Fünfziger Jahre* (Rowohlt, Hamburg, 1983), p. 250.
7. Helen Jones in Sally Placksin, *Jazzwomen: 1900 to the Present: Their Words, Lives and Music* (Pluto Press, London and Sydney, 1985), pp. 142–3.
8. See 'Jazz im Rundfunk', *Funk Illustrierte*, 14 (1949), p. 4.
9. 'Der alteste Hahn ist tot' (The oldest cock is dead), *Der Spiegel*, 13 October 1949, p. 39.

Chapter eight: Coca-Cola and Cars: Icons of the American Dream

1. The song in the campaign was 'I was raised on country sunshine'. The opening of the final chapter of Bill Malone's classic survey of country music is relevant:

    Country music's history since the early seventies has been one of unqualified commercial success . . . The country music industry

has discovered that its best interests lie in the distribution of a
package with clouded identity, possessing no regional traits . . . a
music that is all things to all people: middle-of-the-road and
'American' . . .
Bill C. Malone, *Country Music USA*, revised edition, Austin,
Texas: University of Texas Press, 1985, p. 369.

2. Helmut Fritz, *Coca-Cola: Das Evangelium der Erfrischung* Siegen:
   MUK 9, 1980, p. 4.
3. 'Feuchte Stimme Amerikas' (Damp voice of America), *Der Spiegel*,
   13 July 1950, p. 28.
4. 'Sport was also crucial to a complex of themes which the Nazis
   wished to appropriate – health, youth, preparedness, competition,
   etc . . . The triumphs of German sport, in football, boxing,
   motor-racing and athletics were also triumphs of the 'new'
   Germany.'
   Martin Chalmers, 'Notes on Nazi propaganda', *Screen Education*
   40, Autumn/Winter (1981–2): 36–7.
5. Quoted in J. C. Louis and Harvey Z. Yazijian, *The Cola Wars*,
   New York: Everest House, 1980, p. 75.
6. ibid., p. 99.
7. Quoted in Reyner Banham, 'Europe and American design', in R.
   Rose (ed.) *Lessons From America*, London: Macmillan, 1974,
   p. 69.
8. ibid., p. 73.
9. Jeffrey Herf, 'The engineer as ideologue: reactionary modernists in
   Weimar and Nazi Germany', *Journal of Contemporary History* 19
   (1984): 640, 635.
10. John Heskett, 'Modernism and archaism in design in the Third
    Reich', *Block* 3 (1980): 21.
11. Paul Maenz, *Art Deco 1920–1940*, Köln: DuMont Schauberg, 1974,
    p. 197.
12. See Dick Hebdige, 'Towards a cartography of taste 1935–1962',
    Block 4 (1981): 39–56 and Banham, 'Europe and American design',
    p. 85.
13. These were to be the principal icons in Tom Wesselman's Pop
    painting of 1963, 'Still Life No. 34'.
14. The 10,000th Volkswagen, made in 1946, was covered by the
    factory workers with scrawled messages asking for '*mehr und
    schmackhafteres Essen*' (more and tastier food).

Chapter nine: The 1950s: Cold War / Hot Sun in Capri

1. 'Currency reform established overnight the new society, the society
   of capitalism. And immediately in a very modern form: of mass
   production and consumption, of marketing and the satisfaction of
   economic needs.' Carl Amery (1963), cited in Gordon A. Craig,
   The Germans, Harmondsworth: Penguin, 1984, p. 123.

2. Jean Baudrillard, *La Société de Consommation*, Paris: Gallimard, 1970 (reprinted 1976), p. 195.
3. See the introduction by myself and Stephen Baskerville to *Nothing Else to Fear: New Perspectives on America in the Thirties*, Manchester: Manchester University Press, 1985, especially pp. 6–7: 'By its commitment to the preservation of capitalism the New Deal was also committed to sustaining and expanding a consumer economy to which the social uses of technology were central.'
4. Frank W. Fox, *Madison Avenue Goes to War: The Strange Military Career of American Advertising 1941–45*, Provo, Utah: Brigham Young University Press, 1975, p. 96.
5. In *Germany Today: A Personal Report* (London: Weidenfeld and Nicholson, 1985), Walter Laqueur observes that the modern German village has less in common with the pre-war village than with the modern German town:

    The shops had a surprisingly rich selection of goods, there were public call boxes at the corners, television aerials on every roof, car ownership was universal . . . I met one successful farmer, owner of a substantial herd of dairy cows who confessed that he did not know how to milk a cow by hand (pp. 26–7).
6. See Peter Rühmkorf's poem 'Variations on "Song of a German" by Friedrich Hölderlin'.
7. Ursula Wassermann, *I Was an American*, London: Lane, 1955, p. 188.
8. Hans Spier, *From the Ashes of Disgrace: A Journal From Germany, 1944–55*, Amherst: University of Massachusetts Press, 1981, p. 96.
9. H. Abosch, *The Menace of the Miracle: Germany from Hitler to Adenauer*, New York: Monthly Review Press, 1963, p. 109.
10. Joyce Rheuban, Introduction, *The Marriage of Maria Braun* [Rainer Werner Fassbinder, director], New Brunswick, New Jersey: Rutgers University Press, 1986, p. 8.
11. S. Gohr, 'Art in the Post-War Period', in C.M. Joannides, N. Rosenthal and W. Schmied (eds) *German Art in the Twentieth Century: Painting and Sculpture 1905–1985*, London: Royal Academy of Arts, 1985, p. 467.
12. Abosch, *The Menace of the Miracle*, p. 107.
13. Jost Hermand, 'Modernism restored: West German painting in the 1950s', *New German Critique* 32 (Spring/Summer) (1984): 23–41.
14. Erica Carter, 'Alice in the consumer wonderland: West German case studies in gender and consumer culture', in Angela McRobbie and Mica Nava (eds) *Gender and Generation*, London: Macmillan, 1984, pp. 190, 199.
15. 'Germany: untidy and brutal', *Die Welt (Holland)*, 26 February 1957.
16. Laqueur, *Germany Today*, p. 113. The description of McDonald's is by Wolfgang Pohrt, cited in Laqueur, p. 164.

17. Quitt in Peter Handke, *They are Dying Out*, London: Methuen, 1975, Act I, p. 11.
18. David Lodge, *Out of the Shelter*, Harmondsworth: Penguin, 1986, Afterword, p. 276.

Select Bibliography

Books

Abosch, H. (1963) *The Menace of the Miracle: Germany From Hitler to Adenauer*, New York: Monthly Review Press.

Allen, J.S. (1983) *The Romance of Commerce and Culture: Capitalism, Modernism and the Chicago-Aspen Crusade for Cultural Reform*, Chicago: University of Chicago Press.

Anderson, B. (1977) 'America in Europe: Interaction of Popular Cultures', unpublished PhD thesis, University of California, Santa Barbara.

Bach, J. (1946) *America's Germany*, New York: Random House.

Barnet, R.J. (1983) *Allies: America–Europe–Japan Since the War*, New York: Simon and Schuster.

Berghahn, V. (1986) *The Americanization of West German Industry 1945– 1973*, Leamington Spa: Berg Publishers Ltd.

Bleuel, H.P. (1973) *Strength Through Joy*, London: Secker & Warburg.

Botting, D. (1985) *In the Ruins of the Reich*, London: Allen and Unwin.

Breitenkamp, E. (1953) *The US Information Control Division and its Effects on German Publishers and Writers*, Grand Forks, North Dakota: University Station.

Chamberlin, B.S. (1979) *Kultur auf Trümmern: Berliner Berichte der Amerikanischen Information Control Section, Juli–Dezember, 1945*, Stuttgart.

Corn, J.J. (ed.) (1986) *Imagining Tomorrow; History, Technology and the American Future*, Cambridge, Mass.: MIT Press.

Craig, G.A. (1984) *The Germans*, Harmondsworth: Penguin.

Davidson, E. (1959) *The Death and Life of Germany*, London: Cape.

Davis, F.M. (1967) *Come as a Conqueror: US Army Occupation of Germany 1945–1949*, New York: Macmillan.

Deutsche, K.W. and Edinger, L.J. (1959) *Germany Rejoins the Powers*, Stanford, Calif.: Stanford University Press.

Dollinger, H. (1967) *Deutschland unter den Besatzungsmächten 1945–1949*, Munich: Kurt Desch.

Ehrenfreund, N. (1950) 'The Birth of a New German Press: the Story of Post-War German Newspapers in the US Occupation Area 1945–49', unpublished MA thesis, Columbia University, New York.

Elder, R.E. (1968) *The Information Machine: The US Information Agency and American Foreign Policy*, New York: Syracuse University Press.

Fielding, R. (1972) *The American Newsreel, 1911–1967*, Norman, Oklahoma: University of Oklahoma Press.

Fox, F.W. (1975) *Madison Avenue Goes to War: The Strange Military Career of American Advertising 1941–45*, Provo, Utah: Brigham Young University Press.

Fritz, H. (1980) *Coca-Cola: Das Evangelium der Erfrischung*, Siegen: MUK 9.

Fulbright, Senator J. (1970) *The Pentagon Propaganda Machine*, New York: Vintage Books.

Gaiser, G. (1960) *The Last Dance of the Season* (Schlussball) (trans. M. Waldman), London: Collins.

Galantiere, L. (1951) *America and the Mind of Europe*, London: Hamish Hamilton.

Gimbel, J. A. (1961) *A German Community under Occupation: Marburg 1945–52*, Stanford, Calif.: Stanford University Press.

Glaser, H. (1986) *The Rubble Years: The Cultural Roots of Post-War Germany 1945–48*, New York: Paragon House.

Gross, F.B. (1952) 'Freedom of Press under the Military Government in West Germany 1945–49', unpublished PhD, Harvard University, Cambridge, Mass.

Guback, T.H. (1960) *The International Film Industry*, Bloomington: Indiana University Press.

Habe, H. (1953) *Our Love Affair with Germany*, New York: Putnam.

Hartemann, L.R. (1984) 'Propaganda and the Control of Information in Occupied Germany: The US Information Control Division at Radio Frankfurt 1945–49', unpublished PhD, Rutgers University at New Brunswick, New Jersey.

Hartrich, E. (1980) *The Fourth and Richest Reich*, New York: Collier-Macmillan.

Henderson, J.W. (1969) *The United States Information Agency*, New York: Praeger.

Higham, C. (1983) *Trading with the Enemy: An Exposé of the Nazi-American Money Plot 1933–1949*, London: Hale.

Hurwitz, H. (1972) *Die Stunde Null der deutschen Presse: Die amerikanische Pressepolitik in Deutschland (1945–49)*, Köln: Verlag Wissenschaft und Politik.

Kolko, J. and G. (1972) *The Limits of Power: The World and US Foreign Policy 1945–53*, New York: Harper and Row.

Krippendorf, E. (ed.) (1981) *The Role of the US in the Reconstruction of Italy and West Germany 1943–1949*, Berlin: Materialien 16, J.F. Kennedy Institut, Freie Universitat.

Kvam, W.E. (1973) *Hemingway in Germany: The Fiction, the Legend and the Critics*, Athens, Ohio: University of Ohio Press.

Laqueur, W. (1985) *Germany Today: A Personal Report*, London: Weidenfeld and Nicholson.

Litchfield, E.H. (ed.) (1953) *Governing Post War Germany*, Ithaca, New York: Cornell University Press.

Lodge, D. (1986) *Out of the Shelter*, Harmondsworth: Penguin.

Louis, J.C. and Yazijian, H.Z. (1980) *The Cola Wars*, New York: Everest House.

Lukacs, J. (1978) *1945: Year Zero*, New York: Doubleday, Garden City.

MacCann, R.D. (1973) *The People's Films: A Political History of US Government Motion Pictures*, New York: Hastings House.

McClelland, C.E. and Scher, S.P. (eds) (1974) *Postwar German Culture: An anthology*, New York: Dutton.

Maginnis, J.J. (1971) *Military Government Journal: Normandy to Berlin*, Amherst, Mass.: University of Massachusetts Press.

Mattelart, A. (1979) *Multinational Corporations and the Control of Culture: The Ideological Apparatuses of Imperialism*, Brighton: Harvester.

Merritt, A.J. and R.L. (1970) *Public Opinion in Occupied Germany: The OMGUS Surveys, 1945–1949*, Urbana, Illinois: University of Illinois Press.

Mettler, B. (1975) *Demokratisierung-und Kalter Krieg. Zur amerikanischen Informations und Rundfunkpolitik in W. Deutschland 1945–49*, Berlin: Spiess.

Norman A. (1951) *Our German Policy: Propaganda and Culture*, New York: Vantage Press.

Padover, S. (1946) *Experiment in Germany*, New York: Duell, Sloan Pearce.

Paulu, B. (1967) *Radio and Television Broadcasting on the European Continent*, Minneapolis: University of Minnesota Press.

Petersen, E.N. (1978) *Retreat to Victory: The American Occupation of Germany*, Detroit, Michigan: Wayne State University Press.

Peterson, T. (1964) *Magazines in the Twentieth Century*, Urbana: University of Illinois Press.

Pilgert, H.P. (1951) *The History of the Development of Information Services through Information Centers and Documentary Films*, Historical Division Office of the Executive Secretary, Office of the US High Commission for Germany.

—— (1953) *Press, Radio and Film in West Germany, 1945–1953*, Historical Division, Office of the US High Commission for Germany.

Pronay, N. and Wilson, K. (eds) (1985) *The Political Re-Education of Germany and Her Allies after World War II*, London/Sydney: Croom Helm.

Pross, H. (ed.) (1965) *Deutsche Presse seit 1945*, Bern: Scherz.

Report to the Congress, *Telling America's Story to the World – Problems and Issues: United States Information Agency*, Washington, DC: Comptroller General of the United States.

Rodnick, D. (1948) *Postwar Germans*, New Haven, Conn.: Yale University Press.

Ruhl, K.-J. (1980) *Die Besatzer und die Deutschen, Amerikanische Zone 1945–48*, Düsseldorf: Droste.

Rundell Jr, W. (1964) *Black Market Money*, Baton Rouge: Louisiana State University Press.

Schafer, H.D. (1981) *Das gespaltene Bewusstsein: Deutsche Kultur und Lebenswirklichkeit 1933–1945*, München-Wien: Hanser.

Schalluck, P. (ed.) (1971) *Germany: Cultural Developments Since 1945*, Munich: Max Hueber Verlag.

Schiller, H.I. (1969) *Mass Communications and American Empire*, New York: Augustus M. Kelley.

Sedgwick, M. (1979) *The Motor Car 1946–56*, London: Batsford.

Settel, A. (1950) *This is Germany*, New York: Sloane.

Siepmann, E. (ed.) (1983) *Bikini, die fünfziger Jahre: Kalter Krieg und Capri-Sonne*, Hamburg: Rowohlt.

Sorenson, T.C. (1968) *The Word War: The Story of American Propaganda*, New York: Harper and Row.

Speier, H. (1981) *From the Ashes of Disgrace: A Journal From Germany 1945–55*, Amherst: University of Massachusetts Press.

Tent, J.F. (1983) *Mission on the Rhine: Reeducation and Denazification in American Occupied Germany*, Chicago: University of Chicago Press.

Thomson, C.A.H. (1948) *Overseas Information Service of the US Government*, Washington, DC: The Brookings Institution.

Trommler, F. and McVeigh, J. (eds) (1985) *America and the Germans: An Assessment of a 300-Year History, Vol. 2, The Relationship in the Twentieth Century*, Philadelphia: University of Pennsylvania Press.

Turner Jr, H.A. (1987) *The Two Germanies, since 1945*, New Haven: Yale University Press.

United States Senate (1973) *Radio Free Europe and Radio Liberty: Hearings before the Committee on Foreign Relations (S.1914)*, Washington, DC: US Government Printing Office.

Wassermann, U. (1955) *I Was an American*, London: Lane.

Watters, P. (1978) *Coca-Cola: An Illustrated History*, New York: Doubleday.

Whitton, J.B. (ed.) (1963) *Propaganda and the Cold War*, Washington, DC: Public Affairs Press.

Wilder, T. (1962) *Our Town and Other Plays*, Harmondsworth: Penguin.

Wood, J.P. (1967) *Of Lasting Interest: The Story of the Reader's Digest*, Garden City, New York: Doubleday.

Woodruff, W. (1975) *America's Impact on the World*, London: Macmillan.

Ziemke, E.F. (1975) *The US Army in the Occupation of Germany 1944– 46*, Washington, DC: Center of Military History (US Army).

Zink, H. (1957) *The US in Germany 1944–1955*, Princeton, New Jersey: Van Nostrand.

Zwerin, M. (1985) *La Tristesse de Saint Louis: Swing under the Nazis*, London: Quartet.

Periodical articles

Annals of the American Academy of Political and Social Science (1948) November, 'Postwar Reconstruction in Western Germany'.

Asman, J. (1978) 'Jazz and the jackboot', *Jazz Circle News* 9, October: 8–9, 16.

Banham, R. (1974) 'Europe and American design', in Rose, R. (ed.), *Lessons from America*, London: Macmillan 67–91.

Berendt, J.E. (1962) 'Jazz in Germany', *Down Beat*, 11 October: 22–3.

Blake, P. (1957) 'German architecture and America', *Architectural Forum* 107, August: 133–5.

Bungestab, K.-E. (1971) 'Entstehung, Bedeutungs- und Funktionswandel der Amerika-Häuser. Ein Beitrag zur Geschichte der amerikanischen Auslandsinformation nach dem 2. Weltkrieg', *Jarhbuch für Amerikastudien* 16: 189–203.

Chalmers, M. (1986) 'Swingtime for Hitler', *New Musical Express*, 8 September: 20–1.

Conrad, G. (1971) 'Rex Stewart in Berlin', *Jazz Journal* 24(3): 13–4.

Coser, L.A. (1948) 'Germany, 1948', *Commonweal*, 11 June: 208–11.

'Feuchte Stimme Amerikas' (Damp voice of America) (1950) *Der Spiegel*, 13 July: 28–30.

Frenz, H. (1960) 'The Reception of Thornton Wilder's Plays in Germany', *Modern Drama*, III, 2: 123–37.

Frey, J.R. (1955) 'Postwar German reactions to American literature', *Journal of English and Germanic Philology* LIV: 173–94.

Fussell Jr, P. (1958) 'Thornton Wilder and the German psyche', *The Nation*, 3 May: 394–5.

Gaither, M. and Frenz, H. (1955) 'German criticism of American drama', *American Quarterly*, VII(2): 111–22.

Gimbel, J. (1965) 'Artificial revolution in Germany', *Political Science Quarterly* March: 88–104.

Gohr, S. (1985) 'Art in the post-war period', in C.M. Joannides, N. Rosenthal, and W. Schmied (eds) *German Art in the Twentieth Century: Painting and Sculpture 1905–1985*, London: Royal Academy of Arts.

Guback, T. (1986) 'Shaping the film business in postwar Germany: the role of the US film industry and the US state', in P. Kerr (ed.) *The Hollywood Film Industry*, London: Routledge and Kegan Paul.

Hebdige, D. (1981) 'Towards a cartography of taste 1935–1962', *Block* 4: 39–56.

Hermand, J. (1984) 'Modernism restored: West German painting in the 1950's, *New German Critique* 32 (Spring/Summer): 23–41.

Hoenisch, M. (1982) 'Film as an instrument of the US re-education program in Germany after 1945 and the example of *Todesmühlen'*, *Englisch– Amerikanische Studien* 1–2, (Juni): 196–210.

Institut für Auslandsbeziehungen Stuttgart (1987) 'In der Vergangenheit nach Zukunftsperspektiven Ausschau halten; Die Vereinigten Staaten von Amerika und Deutschland 1945–1950 und danach', *Zeitschrift fur Kulturaustausch* 2: 206–381.

Joffe, J. (1983), 'The greening of Germany', *The New Republic* 14 (February): 18–22.

Kreuter, W. and Oltmann, J. (1984) 'Coca-Cola statt Apfelmost: Kalter Krieg und Amerikanisierung westdeutscher Lebensweise', *Englisch– Amerikanische Studien* 1 (Marz): 22–35.

Lange, W. (1982) 'Die Schaubühne als politische Umerziehungsanstalt betrachet: Theater in den Westzonen', in J. Hermand, H. Peitsch, and K.R. Scherpe (eds) *Nachkriegsliteratur in Westdeutschland, 1945– 49*, Berlin: Argument-Sonderband AS 83: 6–35.

Meier, E. (1954) 'The licensed press in the US Occupation zone of Germany', *Journalism Quarterly* 31: 223–31.

Middleton, D. (1945) 'Germany today: doleful and angry', *New York Times*, 16 September: 10, 11, 27.

Neumann, F.L. (1947) 'Re-educating the Germans: the dilemma of reconstruction', *Commentary* June: 517–25.

Oppel, H. (1962) 'American literature in postwar Germany: impact or alienation?', *Die Neueren Sprachen* 11: 1–10.

Putz, K.H. (1983) 'Business or propaganda? American films and Germany, 1942–1946', *Englisch–Amerikanische Studien* 2–3: 394–414.

Reich, D.R. (1963) 'Accident and design: the reshaping of German broadcasting under military government', *Journal of Broadcasting* 7: 191–207.

Schmied, W. (1985) 'Points of departure and transformations in German art 1905–1985', in C.M. Joannides, N. Rosenthal, and W. Schmied (eds) *German Art in the Twentieth Century: Painting and Sculpture 1905– 1985*, London: Royal Academy of Arts.

Sprager, H.K. (1952) 'Hollywood's foreign correspondents', *Quarterly of Film, Radio and Television* 6: 274–82.

Wagnleitner, R. (1989) 'The irony of American culture abroad: Austria and the Cold War', in L. May (ed.) *Recasting America: Culture and Politics in the Age of Cold War*, Chicago: University of Chicago Press: 285–301.

Wicke, P. (1985) 'Sentimentality and "high pathos": popular music in Fascist Germany', *Popular Music 5: Continuity and Change*, Cambridge: Cambridge University Press: 149–58.

Post-war Chronology

1945

Germany is divided into four Occupation zones to be demilitarized, denazified, and democratized. Radio Munich and stations in Berlin, Frankfurt, and Stuttgart begin broadcasting. The first edition of the newsreel *Welt im Film* is compiled and shown. The first licensed newspaper in the American zone, the *Frankfurter Rundschau*, is published. The culture ministers of the American zone meet to discuss policy. Robert Ardrey's play, *Thunder Rock*, is an outstanding success.

1946

Winston Churchill makes his 'Iron Curtain' speech in Fulton, Missouri. In the American zone elections for city parliaments and county councils are held. Private US citizens are allowed to send food to relief organizations (as well as to relatives and friends in the American zone). The American Military Government holds a conference in Frankfurt to consider youth problems. New magazines include *Der Ruf* and *Frankfurter Hefte*. Licensed magazines and newspapers are permitted to publish information from foreign news agencies. Thornton Wilder's *The Skin of Our Teeth* is staged in Darmstadt and Berlin. Secretary of State James Byrne pledges the US to further the democratic federal and economic reconstruction of Germany.

1947

The American and British zones merge their economic roles to produce 'Bizonia', with Frankfurt designated as capital. The Marshall Plan is announced. *Der Spiegel* prints its first edition.

Gropius visits Germany for a lecture tour. An exhibition of 'Extreme Painting' is opened in Augsburg.

1948

New magazines include *Der Monat*, *Quick*, and *Der Stern*. Currency reform: the introduction of the Deutschmark. The process of ending rations, inflation, and price and salary controls begins. The blockade of West Berlin is initiated and to counter it the British–American airlift is started.

1949

Elections for the first West German Parliament take place and Adenauer becomes first Chancellor of the Federal Republic.

Index

Adenauer, Konrad 104, 116, 122, 148
Americanization; Americanisms 12, 85, 125, 126, 128; in business 7–8, 9, 108, 118, 120, 128; in cabaret 4; CARE packages 2, 46, 65, 84, 129; cigarettes 3, 4, 11, 13, 14, 32, 36, 110–1, 136; consumerism 9–10, 11–12, 26, 75–7, 79, 84, 101, 103, 108–9, 111, 114, 115–22 passim, 125–6, 127, 128, 129, 130; democracy viii 2, 5, 6, 7, 11, 12, 16, 17, 18, 20, 21, 27, 31, 42, 56, 62, 64, 67, 69, 73, 78, 80, 84, 89, 98, 99, 112, 116, 121, 123, 130; in France viii; of German youth 17–18, 19, 122, 125–6, 129, 133; Hollywood 8, 9, 11, 13, 27, 28–9, 32, 33, 34, 35, 40–1, 60, 77, 79, 98, 106, 109, 111, 113, 116, 118, 119, 122; in Italy 28; mass culture 8, 11–12, 13, 67, 74–7, 78, 79, 81, 85, 109, 117, 119, 121–2, 124, 129; of POWs 17; in Weimar 8, 13, 28
architecture 48–53; functionalism 49; restoration 49–50
Ardrey, Robert 62, 65, 147; Thunder Rock 65, 68–9, 70, 147
Arthur, Jean 34–5

Baudrillard, Jean 115–16
Bauhaus 49, 50, 106, 108
Bavaria 1, 3, 4, 5, 14
Berlin 3, 8, 13, 14, 19, 22, 23, 26, 30, 31, 33–9 passim, 42–3, 46, 49, 53, 67, 72, 79, 80, 82, 84, 90, 93, 94, 95, 96–7, 98, 101, 105, 119, 121, 147, 148
Best Years of Our Lives, The 29, 80–1, 118
Bild–Zeitung 124
black market 30, 31, 32, 33, 36–7, 42, 43, 77, 87, 125, 126
books 55–6; absence of 54
Bundesrepublik see Federal Republic

Capra, Frank 25, 35, 67, 79, 106, 117; It Happened One Night 106; Mr Deeds Goes to Town 35, 67, 79; Mr Smith Goes to Washington 29, 35; Why We Fight 17
Coca-Cola viii 8, 11, 12–13, 76, 79, 81, 99–105, 121, 123, 125, 129, and Plate 1
Cold War 2, 11, 17, 18, 21–2, 24, 26, 27, 38, 69–70, 78, 80, 82, 91, 100, 103–109, 114, 121, 123
currency reform 11, 110, 115, 118, 127, 138, 148

Dietrich, Marlene 33, 35–6, 38–9

Evarts, John 61, 69;
memorandum 71–2

Federal Republic 2, 9, 11, 12, 14, 38, 52, 85, 100, 104, 111, 120, 121, 122, 124, 127, 132, 136, 148
film 28–44; documentary 24–7, 28; *Autobiography of a Jeep* 112–13; *Between East and West* 26; *The Bridge* 26; *It's Up To You* 26; *Made in Germany* 26; *Streetcar Called Freedom* 27; *Step by Step* 26; *Todesmühlen* 38; *TVA* 25; *Two Cities* 26; *Why We Fight* see Capra
Ford 7, 113, 116
Ford, Henry 9, 89, 113
Frankfurt 4, 5–6, 8, 18, 19, 23, 48, 50, 52, 63, 79, 88, 89, 94, 96, 105, 109, 112, 118, 147

GDR 92, 97, 119
GIs ix 1, 3, 4, 13, 18, 32–3, 34, 38, 42, 77, 79, 80, 81, 88, 90, 91, 94, 102, 104, 105, 111, 126; fraternization 6, 30, 42, 93, 135
Goebbels, Joseph 8, 107, 128
Gropius, Walter 49, 50, 51, 106, 108, 148

Half-time (Walser) 128–9
Heimat 67; *Heimatfilme* 119, 121, 124; *Heimatlieder* 92
Heldt, Werner 46
Hellman, Lilian 61, 71; *Watch on the Rhine* 61
Hemingway Ernest 55, 56, 57–8, 69; *For Whom the Bell Tolls* 56, 57, 58
Hindemith, Paul 23
Hitler, Adolf 8, 88, 89, 91, 107, 113, 127
Hofer, Karl 46
How German Is It (Abish) 127

Jazz 8, 12, 13, 18, 84, 85, 86–98, 104, 109, 132; bebop 93, 98;

Edelhagen, Kurt 91, 94, 96; Gillespie, Dizzy 98; Goodman, Benny 86, 87, 90; International Sweethearts of Rhythm 95; Kenton, Stan 94, 96, 97; Lubo D'Orio band 87, 94; Miller, Glenn 90, 94, 95; New Orleans jazz 93–4; on radio 95, 104; post-war records 96, 97; Stewart, Rex 96–7; swing 5, 86–88 *passim*, 90, 92, 94, 95; *Swing Jugend* 88–90; Waller, Fats 86, 88, 89
Jeep, (Willys) 112
Jones, James 58, 59–60; *From Here to Eternity* 58, 59–60

Kahlschlag 48, 57
Keith, Max 100–4 *passim*

Last Dance of the Season, (Gaiser) 127–8
Lodge, David x 50, 130; *Out of the Shelter* 50, 130
Loewy, Raymond 110, 111, 112

magazines; *Die Amerikanische Rundschau* 54, 81; *Bravo* 126; *Frankfurter Rundschau* 3, 49, 73, 147; *Heute* 74, 80, 81, 83–4, 98; *Life* 73–81 *passim*, 84, 112, 117, 123, 137; *Der Monat* 5, 82, 119, 148; *Neue Auslese* 74, 81, 83; *Neue Zeitung* 3, 5, 70, 82–3; *Reader's Digest* 74, 78, 81, 117; *Der Ruf* 2–3, 57, 147; *Saturday Evening Post* 17, 75, 76, 79, 117; *Der Spiegel* 14, 81, 85, 98, 106, 113, 137, 138, 147; *Time* 11, 12, 37, 73–8 *passim*, 81, 85, 118, 136
Mailer, Norman 58–9; *The Naked and the Dead* 58–9
Marburg 1–2, 20, 132
Marriage of Maria Braun, The 122, 125
Marshall Plan 2, 11, 26, 49, 98, 103, 126, 147

Miller, Arthur 12, 61, 71; *All My Sons* 61, 71, 72; *Death of a Salesman* 60
Munich 4, 5, 19, 23, 46, 60, 83, 92, 118, 147; 'Munich Mountaineers' 91

Odets, Clifford 61, 71; *Awake and Sing!* 60, 61
OMGUS 3, 7, 14, 20, 21, 22, 27, 28–9, 33, 48, 49, 61, 67, 74, 83, 84, 147

Painting 45–8, 122–3, 148; abstract expressionism 123; abstraction 47–8, 122; magic realism 47
plastic 110, 111–12
Porsche, Ferdinand 107, 108, 112

Re-education viii 5, 11, 14, 16–27, 32, 33, 38, 40, 58, 61, 62, 64, 129; America Houses (USICs) 5, 18, 19–24, 62, 91; American Studies 19; denazification 7, 8, 57, 61, 92, 147; OWI 16, 24–5, 29, 30, 31–2, 73, 74, 84, 102, 112, 134, 147; universities 18–19, 45; *Welt im Film* 6, 15, 24
Rowohlt, Ernst 54, 56
Rühmkorf, Peter 102, 120

Scharoun, Hans 49, 53
Silk Stockings 126
Skidmore, Owings and Merrill 51–2
Steinbeck, John 56, 60, 83

streamlining 12, 76, 108–9, 110–1, 112, 113
Stunde Null see Zero Hour

Tessenow, Heinrich 49
They Are Dying Out (Handke) 129

Van der Rohe, Mies 50–2 *passim*, 106
Van Druten, John 64, 98; *I Remember Mama* 64–5; *The Voice of the Turtle* 65–6
von Rebay, Hilla 45–6

Wenders, Wim 4–5, 130
Wilder, Billy 25, 29–44; *A Foreign Affair* 30–44; 'Propaganda through Entertainment' 29–30, 40–4, and Plates 2 and 3
Wilder, Thornton 12, 29, 62, 119, 147; *Our Town* 62, 66–7, 70, 84; *The Skin of Our Teeth* 12, 66, 67–8, 147
Williams, Tennessee 12, 61; *The Glass Menagerie* 60; *A Streetcar Named Desire* 60
Wolfe, Thomas 56, 60, 83; *You Can't Go Home Again* 56
Women, role of 124–5
Wright, Frank Lloyd 50, 83
Wrigley's gum 104

Zero Hour viii 4, 11, 55, 57, 58, 122
Zuckmayer, Carl 63; *The Captain of Köpenick* 121; *The Devil's General* 63